# Morning Glory

## A 52-WEEK DEVOTIONAL

YOLANDA D. TURNER

yblala63@gmail.com
Tanner, AL

NU BEGINNINGS, LLC

Editing by Cara Highsmith - Highsmith Creative Services

www.highsmithcreative.com

Cover and Interior Design by Mitchell Shea

ISBN 978-1-7323309-0-0

Printed in the United States of America

First Edition 14 13 12 11 10 / 10 9 8 7 6 5 4 3 2 1

# MORNING GLORY
# DEVOTIONAL

Dedicated to
My Heavenly Father.
Your pursuing love and amazing grace
saved my life;

and

to all the overcomers in the body of Christ Jesus;
let your testimonies be living proof of God's mighty acts.

# Foreword

There are moments in life that shape us and help define who we are or will become. They're not always earth-shattering or even recognizable as particularly important at the time. But as we age and our souls look back, it becomes clear that but for that one moment in time, we would not have made it over life's inevitable obstacles, pains, heartaches, and disappointments.

One of my most pertinent moments happened in the summer of 1976. It was my first full summer with Granny. I stayed with her once my mother started her career as a registered nurse. Kindergarten was a distant year away and daycare centers were rarities in an era where elder matriarchs filled every neighborhood and willingly took charge of the "village" children.

"It's time to pray, Sugar," Granny said softly. Her good-natured wit was substituted with an unfamiliar seriousness. It was obvious I had no say in the matter, so I knelt beside her without protest. Granny cupped my small hand in hers and held it to the television screen, right up to the enlarged face of televangelist Oral Roberts. This wasn't the first time I'd ever prayed. My parents insisted that I give God a laundry list of people to bless each night before climbing into bed. But this experience was different. Somehow, some way, Granny was literally talking to God.

With one eye closed and the other shifting between Granny and the television, I was intrigued by this man who was reaching out to us from the screen, calling down the power of Jesus Christ and driving Granny to tears.

"Thank you, Jesus," she finally said, just above a whisper. She raised herself up, pulling me with her, wiped her eyes, and turned off the television just as the closing program credits started to roll.

"What's wrong, Granny?" I asked.

"Nothing, Sugar. I'm just happy, that's all," she said as she took me into the kitchen to indulge in a fresh-baked pan of homemade rolls laced with melted butter.

Grown-ups had a funny way of being happy, I thought.

I moved from that summer as a vivacious five-year-old, intrigued by the ritual of prayer, to being a spiritually impatient teenager. At my local church, the pastor opened the service with prayer, followed by a prayer from the deacons, then on to altar prayer, where, at any given moment, someone was going to get "happy," run a short marathon around the church and fall to the floor, thus extending service by a good thirty minutes.

"Why does church have to last so long?" I whined in pubescent agitation, careful not to cross any boundaries that might cause a powerful and painful rebuke from my parents. "Is all that crying and carrying on really necessary?"

"One day you'll understand, Sugar," Granny said from her bedside, where her tired and ailing body was now forced to stay most days.

As Granny predicted, one day came.

I imagine this Christian walk to be like a WWE wrestling match. Life tosses you to and fro, body slams you, and puts you in a sleeper hold. Once you're down, the devil hovers over you like a referee, counting down, ready to declare your defeat. And the whole time from the corner of your eye, you see God on the sidelines waiting for you to tap Him in so He can take over the fight.

But how do you reach God when your situation makes Him look so far off? What do you do when your back is against the ropes and you must truly decide to walk by faith and not by sight—where you are forced to believe that God is with you and has not forsaken you and that He will supply all of your needs in a time of spiritual, emotional, or financial drought? You do it through prayer and the study of His Word.

This is why resources like *The Morning Glory Devotional*, are so important for your daily walk. With over ten years of dedicated service in children's and women's ministry, Yolanda reminds us that we tap into God by tapping into His word, and she has provided a unique way of incorporating that into our daily lives. In powerful and inspirational devotions, Yolanda recounts through examples from her personal life experiences how God has shown up in her life to guide her, give her relief, and secure her victory over the challenges she has wrestled with along the way. You will see through her story how her unwavering faith in God carried her through domestic violence, divorce, poverty, and single parenting. Her testimony is supported by daily scriptures that provide encouragement and strength. And the additional tools and insights she includes offer a multi-faceted and multi-layered approach to inviting God into our daily lives and remind us that nothing can separate us from the love of God or His promises. No fight is too hard for Him. He's just waiting for us to tap Him in!

Rita Roberts-Turner

# INTRODUCTION

For years I struggled with trying to find the perfect time to do daily devotion throughout the course of a day. That changed when I surrendered to being awakened in the early hours of the morning by the Spirit to pray and to read the Bible. I found that during these early morning wake-up calls I had no interruptions, my mind was free from random thoughts, and I was well-rested for devotion. This newfound time of devotion was like a fresh cup of coffee that set a positive atmosphere for the day. My appointed time allowed me to give God my very best devotion, and starting my day with Him set me up for the best possible outcomes.

I have no difficulty getting up earlier to start my day with devotion. I greet my God with, *Morning Glory, Father give me a word through my devotional Bible reading that will guide me today*. When a particular scripture is illuminated in my heart, I know without a doubt it is my guiding word for that day.

One morning during my devotional time, the promptings of the Holy Spirit touched my heart to share the godly inspired scripture and prayer with every person willing to receive it through texting. So, I changed my prayer to: *Morning Glory, Father give me a word for today to share with your people—a word of healing, peace, joy, and hope*. I began texting the scriptures and prayers every morning during the early hours with the crowing of the rooster. For many, the scriptures and prayers have become their morning wake-up call to the glorious message of God's timely word. I am thankful to have six hundred followers receiving the daily scriptures and prayers that God leads me to share with them.

I have a heart for God and I love his Word! I'm not a theologian or biblical scholar. I didn't come from riches or fame, but I am a Child of God who is in pursuit of God's heart. God healed me from terminal illness, saved me from abusive relationships, and delivered me from depression, low self-esteem, shame, rejection, and betrayal. God opened my spiritual eyes and exposed the true condition of my heart. He purged all of my brokenness, making me whole in Him.

The Word of God transformed my self-hatred to self-love, allowing me to experience his "Agape Love" and to see my true identity proclaimed in God's spoken word that says I'm "fearfully and wonderfully made." The counsel of God's Word freed me from the bondage of Satan's deception that was meant to destroy my life.

I was inspired by God to write this unique devotional study and journal that feature 52-weeks of Bible verses and a daily study outline that will aid you in digging deeper into God's Word. The commentary provides the narrative for the study. I encourage you to keep a journal handy (whether the *Morning Glory Journal* or another notebook) for recording your innermost thoughts and for answering the reflection questions, which are designed to help you check your learning. My intention was to offer a Bible-based devotional that provides guidance and encouragement for life's challenges through weekly prayers, praise songs, and scriptures leading you to God's promises. I've also included additional cross-reference scriptures for further study of God's Word.

My prayer is that this devotional will increase your knowledge and understanding of God's Word and strengthen your faith, anchoring you deeper in God's Word and His promises for you.

Yolanda D. Turner

# CONTENTS

# Week 1

## THE INSEPARABLE LOVE OF GOD WORKING ON YOUR BEHALF

**Morning Glory Devotion**
"And we know that in all things God works for the good of those who love him, who have been called according to his purpose." (Romans 8:28)

**Growing in God's Word**
This scripture became very real and personal to me through my struggles in life, especially during the many years of financial hardship. All of my bills were due the first of every month: mortgage, car notes, groceries, light bills, household expenditures, and many other necessities for my daughters and me. I was a divorcée with limited income and often found myself making partial payments in order to meet all of my monthly obligations. This scripture in particular helped me realize there wasn't anything that would cause God to turn His back on me. So, one day, as I was agonizing over my bills, I clearly heard the Holy Spirit ask me this question, "Yolanda is there anything that would keep you from trusting in Me, regardless of your situation?" I responded without hesitation, *No, Father God, there is nothing that would ever cause me to walk away from you or stop me from loving you. Lord, my prayer is that you keep me in the palms of your hands and let nothing and no one snatch me from your hands, not even myself.* The good news is that after my proclamation to God, I never again worried that my bills wouldn't be paid, and I knew God was making the provisions for us.

**Digging Deeper into the Word** (Romans 8:26-39)

DAY 1: God's Provisions (Romans 8:26-28)
- The Holy Spirit intercedes on our behalf to make provision for our needs. (v26a)
- Even when you don't know how to pray, God still hears you. (v26b)
- Jesus intercedes on your behalf. (v26c)
- Jesus aligns your needs with the will of God for your life. (v27)
- All things work out for the good of those who believe. (v28a)
- Provisions come for those who live in accordance with God's purpose and will for their lives. (v28b)

DAY 2: God's Preordained Righteousness (Romans 8:29-34)
- Being chosen means being the offspring of Jesus. (v29)
- We are justified through the blood of Jesus. (v30-34)

DAY 3: God's Faithfulness (Romans 8:35-37)
- Your circumstances don't change God's heart toward you. (v35-36)
- We are victors in Christ (v37)

DAY 4: God's Love/Grace Endures (Romans 8:38-39)
- We can have confidence in God's saving grace. (v38)
- God's love/grace enables us to withstand the challenges of life. (v39)

DAY 5: *Tilling the Heart*

Q1: How do you pray for the things you need?

Q2: What is intercessory prayer? Do you allow the Holy Spirit to intercede on your behalf? If so, how?

Q3: How do you define predestination as it pertains to verse 29?

Q4: How do you define justification? God's righteousness?

Q5: What or who has caused you to separate from the things of God? Explain how.

**Flowering in the Promises of God**
"Let the beloved of the LORD rest secure in him, for he shields

him all day long, and the one the LORD loves rests between his shoulders." (Deuteronomy 33:12)

**Morning Glory Prayer**
*Heavenly Father, thank you for all the provisions you have made and are continuing to make on behalf of my family and me. I thank you for your everlasting love and grace, which is inseparable. I thank you for not allowing life's challenges to separate me from your love and grace. Today, I declare that I am more than a conqueror in all things through Christ Jesus. In Jesus' name I pray, Amen.*

**Tending to the Roots**
Romans 8:26-39

**Nourishing with Praise**
Citizens & Saints – "The Mighty Hand of God"
Jason Nelson – "Nothing Without You"
Calvary Worship ft. Rick Botello – "Alive in Your Light"
Ethan Kent & Bre Botello – "Union"
Trin-i-tee 5:7 – "Over & Over"

**Bringing in the Harvest**
Matthew 6: 25-34, John 14:13-17, Proverbs 4: 23, Philippians 4:19, Jeremiah 17:9-10, Ephesians 1:1-13

# Week 2

## THE WORD THAT STANDS FOREVER

**Morning Glory Devotion**

"For, 'All men are like grass, and all their glory is like the flowers of the field; the grass withers and the flowers fall, but the word of the Lord stands forever.' And this is the word that was preached to you." (1 Peter 1:24-25)

**Growing in God's Word**

I wondered, *How will I ever escape this life of disappointment, broken relationships, abuse, and financial lack?* There was a period when I was living in a state of hopelessness, and I just could not see a way out. I had to change the way I saw myself, my thoughts, and the words I spoke over my life. They didn't line up with or confirm God's Word and promises.

One of the ways I was not aligning with God was in how I lost hope and allowed fear to lead me. I felt stuck in a recurring nightmare with two small babies—jobless, afraid to stay, afraid to leave. I went to God in prayer with my exit plan. With confidence I said to my Father in Heaven, *This is the last time he will beat me. I have a plan and it's a sure way out. It's against your word, but it's a way out.* The voice and the prompting of the Holy Spirit said to me, *If you do this, who will take care of your babies? You will lose your freedom.* Even in my desperation, my love for God was deeper than the love I had for myself, and my heart would not allow me to believe that this was my life's destiny, regardless of the circumstances that surrounded me. I decided to wait until the end of the week to execute my plan of escape because of my love for God. I stood steadfast on God's promise of divine protection and that this would indeed be the last time my (then) husband would beat

4

me. Before the week ended, God made a way out that no man could stop. God healed me and delivered me from Satan's evil plots that were meant to destroy my life. God anchored me in His Word that stands forever.

**Digging Deeper into the Word** (1 Peter 1:17-25)

DAY 1: God's Judgment (1 Peter 1:17-18)
- Every man's work will be judged individually by God. (v17a)
- Live a life that honors God. (v17b)
- The temporary things of this world (silver/gold) cannot fulfill your spiritual needs. (v18a)
- Futile promises handed down by your forefathers will not meet your spiritual needs. (v18b)

DAY 2: Bought with a Price (1 Peter 19-20)
- The redemptive power of the blood of Jesus is what saves us. (v19a)
- His blood is a perfect sacrifice offered for our sins. (v19b)
- His sacrifice is the promise of reconciliation manifested. (v20)

DAY 3: The Power of Salvation (1 Peter 1:21-22)
- As a believer, you must confess your faith. (v21)
- His salvation purifies. (v22)

DAY 4: The Everlasting Word of God. (1 Peter 1:23-25)
- You have spiritual rebirth through Jesus. (v23a)
- Salvation is founded on the Eternal Word of God. (v23b-d)
- The Word of God is eternal and imperishable. (v23e)
- A man's life and all of his riches are like a fallen flower. (v24)
- God gives us His enduring Word. (v25)

DAY 5: *Tilling the Heart*
Q1: How do your daily devotion studies help you during life's setbacks?

Q2: During your study, what permanent solution was revealed for your temporary setback?

Q3: What is your understanding of the biblical meaning of purification?

Q4: How has your salvation in Jesus changed your lifestyle?

Q5: How are you speaking life into your situation with the Word of God?

## Flowering in the Promises of God
"The world and its desires pass away, but the man who does the will of God lives forever." (1 John 2:17)

## Morning Glory Prayer
*Heavenly Father, all things of this world are temporary and will fade away. The beautiful, glorious creations of men will fall to the ground like a fallen flower from its vine. I will not let the temporary things of this world cause me grief. Today, I place all of my hope in You and Your eternal Word. In Jesus' name I pray, Amen.*

## Tending to the Roots
1 Peter 1:18-24

## Nourishing with Praise
Charles Jenkins – "My God Is Awesome"
Chris Tomlin – "Good Good Father"
Matt Redman – "10,000 Reasons (Bless the Lord)"
VaShawn Mitchell – "Nobody Greater"
Maurette Brown Clark – "I AM What God Says I AM"

## Bringing in the Harvest
Isaiah 51:12, 1 Corinthians 6:20, John 1:29, Mathew 25:34, Romans 4:24, Hebrews 13:1, John 3:3, Isaiah 40:6

## Week 3

### A WELL-TRAINED CHILD

**Morning Glory Devotion**
"Train a child in the way he should go, and when he is old he will not turn from it." (Proverbs 22: 6)

**Growing in God's Word**
As a young mother, I vowed to train my children according to God's Word, leading by example through my lifestyle. I strongly believe in family prayer and devotion. Whenever there was a need or trouble within our home I would call for a family meeting, which meant family prayer! It was not unusual for my children to see and hear me walking around the house praying and praising God openly. It was in family devotion that my children learned and understood the importance of prayer. There were times when I was so heavily burdened and blinded by tears that I could not hide my emotions from my children. Seeing my uncontrollable crying, my children offered to pray for me!

My first thought was that they were too young to understand how or what to pray for me, and a young child shouldn't be burdened with the prayer concerns of a parent. Before I could tell them no, they lovingly reminded me that we are a family that prays together, and now it was their turn to pray for Mommy. I needed prayer, so I thanked them for praying for me. Their prayers went straight to my heart and to the ears of God. Peace calmed my troubled mind. It wasn't that their prayer was fancy with extravagant words. It was a beautiful and simple prayer of truth. They prayed with pure hearts, not wavering in their faith. Their voices, offering a sincere plea, resonated deep in my spirit and strengthened my faith, which eliminated all of my doubts, giving me full assurance that God would honor their prayers. This was a teachable moment for me through my children! God uses us all regardless of age.

**Digging Deeper into the Word** (Proverbs 22:1-16)

DAY 1: Godly Character (Proverbs 22:1-3)
- A good name is more valuable than riches. (v1)
- Everyone stands in need of God's grace. (v2-3)

DAY 2: Godly Humility (Proverbs 22:4-5)
- The fear of God produces humility and wisdom. (v4)
- Humility keeps us from dangers and traps. (v5)

DAY 3: Godly Instruction (Proverbs 22:6)
- Give your children the right roadmap for life's journey. (v6a)
- They will arrive at the appointed destination. (v6b)

DAY 4: Godly Stewardship (Proverbs 22:7-15)
- Debt ensnares us and keeps us from God's work. (v7)
- Those who abuse power will lose it. (v8)
- Your blessing is determined by your giving. (v9)
- Live a lifestyle that honors God. (v10-14)
- Corrections produce maturity. (v15)

DAY 5: Tilling the Heart
Q1: How has your godly instruction led your children to having a personal relationship with Christ?
Q2: How have your children used what they have learned to encourage you or others in their walk with Christ?
Q:3: How does your lifestyle serve as a godly example for your children?
Q4: What can you do to assist a wayward child to get back on track with God?
Q5: What role do you play in your adult children's spirituality?

## Flowering in the Promises of God

"Children, obey your parents in the Lord, for this is right. 'Honor your father and mother'—which is the first commandment with a promise—'so that it may go well with you and that you may enjoy long life on the earth.'" (Ephesians 6: 1-3)

## Morning Glory Prayer

*Heavenly Father, I vowed to be an example to my children by living and training them according to your Word. You have given my children a teachable spirit and a submissive heart for out-reach and service for your name's sake. Teach us not to discour-age or doubt the faith of our young. God, use us all, regardless of age, let us be examples for all believers to hear in speech, and see in our lifestyle as we share the gospel in purity and truth. Today, continue to pour out your Holy Spirit on the old and the young. Increase your wisdom and understanding of your Word as we continue to grow spiritually in You. In Jesus' name I pray, Amen.*

## Tending to the Roots

Proverbs 22:1-16

## Nourishing with Praise

Tasha Cobb – "Fill Me Up/Overflow"
Smokey Norful – "I Need You Now"
Matt Turner – "One Two Three"
KWSCM-Kids Worship – "A Gift to You"
Bible Adventure Worship – "I Am a Child of God"

## Bringing in the Harvest

Proverbs 4:1-11, Proverbs 9:10, Deuteronomy 4:9, Deuteronomy 6:6-7, Exodus 9:16, Job 17:9, 2 Thessalonians 2:14-15, 2 Timothy 1:9, Philippians 4:8-9

# Week 4

## HEART EXAMINATION

**Morning Glory Devotion**
"Search me, O God, and know my heart; test me and know my anxious thoughts. See if there is any offensive way in me, and lead me in the way everlasting." (Psalms 139: 23-24)

**Growing in God's Word**
When I find myself being very judgmental or easily offended, reacting contrary to God's word, I ask myself this question: Why does this issue cause me to feel this way? Sometimes I need a spiritual self-check, so I take my checklist to God for an open and honest self-examination. I recall a time when someone hurt me and later apologized. I accepted their apology by saying, "I forgive you," but the memory of the offense was still attacking my mind. I prayed, *Why is this, God? Have I really forgiven him? How do I release him and myself from this offense?* My open confession is not for God to know my faults because He ALREADY knows! But it's my submission saying, *God, search me and show me my faults and any offensive ways in me that hinder my relationship with you and others. Reveal the condition of my heart and purge all unrighteousness and prideful motives that reside in me. Test and expose my thoughts of any impurities, Lord. Cleanse and make me whole. Lead me in the way I should go.*

Are you walking in offense and unforgiveness? If so, it may be time for a spiritual self-check. Seek, ask, and obey God's spiritual direction, then apply God's word, repent, and put on a heart of God.

**Digging Deeper into the Word** (Psalms 139:1-24)

DAY 1: God's Astounding Knowledge of Us (Psalms 139:1-6)
- God knows your innermost qualities. (v1)
- He knows your lying down and your uprising. (v2-3)
- He knows your every thought and every word even before you speak them. (v4-6)

DAY 2: God's Omniscience and Omnipresence (Psalms 139:7-18)
- God sees us in all our Circumstances. (v7-12)
- We were fashioned in God's likeness. (v13-14)
- God saw the moment of our conception and the condition under which it transpired. (v15-16)
- God's knowledge and wisdom are limitless. (v17-18)

DAY 3: Our Heart Condition (Psalms 139:19-23)
- Harboring hatred is not God's way. (v19-22)
- God will help us examine our hearts. (v23a-b)
- God, the cardiologist, knows our hearts. (v23c)
- God's will reveals our motives. (v23d)

DAY 4: Test Results (Psalms 139:24)
- God will lead us in our spiritual diagnosis. (v24a)
- God will provide a treatment plan. (v24b)

DAY 5: *Tilling the Heart*
Q1: What is the current spiritual condition of your heart?
Q2: When was your last spiritual heart examination?
Q3: What are some of the symptoms of a bad heart condition?
Q4: What steps are you taking to prevent a spiritual heart attack?
Q5: What spiritual exercises are you doing to promote a good spiritual heart condition?

**Flowering in the Promises of God**
"If we confess our sins, He is faithful and just to forgive us our sins and purify us from all unrighteousness." (1 John 1:9)

**Morning Glory Prayer**
*Heavenly Father, as I self-check the condition of my heart and search my thoughts, test my motives for pride and open my eyes to any offensive ways within me. Lord, reveal my thoughts of unrighteousness and lead me to your righteousness. Today cleanse my heart and my thoughts by the blood of Jesus Christ. In Jesus' name I pray, Amen.*

**Tending to the Roots**
Psalms 139: 1-24

**Nourishing with Praise**
Vicki Yohe – "Because of Who You Are"
JJ. Hairston & Youthful Praise – "You Deserve It"
Kurt Carr – "For Every Mountain"
Tamela Mann – "I Can Only Imagine"

**Bringing in the Harvest**
Jeremiah 12:3, Jeremiah 17:9-10, Jeremiah 23:24, Job 31:4, Psalms 34:7, Psalms 143:10, Proverbs 15:11, Isaiah 66:18, Romans 11:33, Hebrews 4:13

## Week 5

GRACIOUS CONVERSATION

**Morning Glory Devotion**
"Let your conversation always be full of grace, seasoned with salt, so that you may know how to answer everyone." (Colossians 4:6)

**Growing in God's Word**
Have you ever had to defend your faith or defend the legitimacy of the Bible with a quarrelsome person? How did you handle it? If it didn't go so well, no worries; I'm sure you will be given many more opportunities to get it right. And if your faith hasn't been called into question, I can assure you that the day will come where the legitimacy of your faith will be challenged. I have had plenty of opportunities to get it right, praise God! Through my daily devotional studies and prayers, I have sharpened my conversational skills and I am better prepared to answer anyone in defense of my faith, regardless of where they are coming from.

Paul writes in Colossians, "Let your conversation always be full of grace," with the emphasis being on the key words "your conversation" because you are the one in control of your words. With continuous Bible study and prayer, God's wisdom will show you how to respond to difficult people with grace, patience, and compassion.

I have formed lasting relationships with some of the most difficult people I have ever encountered because I wasn't stirred by their words or tone. Now, I'm more intentional in the words I choose to speak when responding to a quarrelsome person. I choose words of encouragement and words that extend God's grace of love and forgiveness. There's no need to debate the Word of God; sharing the Word of God is much more effective. Effective and gracious communication doesn't come haphazardly, but by spiritual preparation through continuous devotional study and prayer.

**Digging Deeper into the Word** (Colossians 4:2-6)

DAY 1: Preparation for Conversational Battle (Colossians 4:2-3)
- Prayer provides foresight and insight. (v2)
- Prayer provides the spiritual answers. (v3)

DAY 2: Productive Dialogue (Colossians 4:4)
- Strive to defend your faith and salvation by confirming it with the Word of God. (v4a)
- Believers respond in a "Christian Manner"—with kindness, respect, and in loving ways, regardless of the person's revealed bias against the truth. (v4b)

DAY 3: A Tactical Approach (Colossians 4:5)
- Only engage in wise dialogue with unbelievers. (v5a)
- Use every opportunity in conversation to teach and plant the Word of God. (v5b)

DAY 4: Decent Conversation (Colossians 4:6)
- Seek to have conversation that clothes (fills a void or a need) one's soul. (v6a)
- Seek to have conversation that preserves or saves one's soul. (v6b)
- Seek to have conversation that's intriguing so they keep coming back for more. (v6c)

DAY 5: *Tilling the Heart*
Q1: How have you prepared yourself for having a gracious conversation with a quarrelsome person?

Q2: What do others see in your life that lets them know you are a Child of God?
Q3: How do you define *Apologetics*?
Q4: What is your defense for your faith?
Q5: How has your conversation led someone to Christ?

**Flowering in the Promises of God**
"Out of his fullness we have all received grace in place of grace already given." (John 1:16)

**Morning Glory Prayer**
*Heavenly Father, put a guard at my mouth that no corruption comes out. Let my conversation be full of kindness, seasoned with salt. Fill my mouth with your words and guide me on how to answer everyone. Let my conversation be words of encouragement and my response gracious. Today I exalt you with my words of praise. In Jesus' name I pray, Amen.*

**Tending to the Roots**
Colossians 4:2-6

**Nourishing with Praise**
Toby Mac – "Speak Life"
Donald Lawrence – "Encourage Yourself"
Jeremy Camp – "Word of Life"
Marvin Sapp – "The Best in Me"
MercyMe – "Word of God Speak"

**Bringing in the Harvest**
Ephesians 4:29, Ephesians 6:8, Acts 14:27, Mark 4:11, 1 Peter 3:15, Mark 9:50

# Week 6

ONE PURPOSE

**Morning Glory Devotion**
"The one who plants and the one who waters have one purpose, and they will each be rewarded according to their own labor. For we are co-workers in God's service; you are God's field, God's building." (1 Corinthians 3:8-9)

**Growing in God's Word**
Having a leadership position with Children's Ministry, I understood the importance of teamwork. This scripture was a wonderful reminder to me that there are no big or little I's, but everyone has a special skill set given to them by God that I like to call gifted hands and voices from God.

The Children's Ministry at our church consisted of a five-member team. We had assignments based on our talents. Our Praise Worshiper set the atmosphere by ushering in the Holy Spirit through song and dancing. The teacher taught the Bible lesson, and the storyteller read stories relating to the Bible lesson in a very theatrical way! The Event Planner planned games and arts and crafts for the children. The Puppeteer would do a skit based on the Bible lesson with singing and dancing puppets. God moved in the hearts of some of the children during Praise and Worship and others through the Word being taught from the Bible lesson.

It takes a team and their individual special talents to reach the people with the Gospel. For others, singing songs that soften the heart or speaking the word prompts the non-believer to accept the gift of Salvation. Although each team member had different talents they all served with one purpose: to teach the Word of God to the children.

**Digging Deeper into the Word** (1 Corinthians 3:1-11)

DAY 1: Lacking Spiritual Comprehension (1 Corinthians 3:1-3)
- Age is not what determines spiritual maturity; it's the skillful usage of the Word. (v1)
- For some, it takes time to grasp basic concepts of the Word of God. (v2)
- Fleshly understanding prevents spiritual conversations. (v3a)
- Childish thinking may prevent understanding. (v3b)

DAY 2: Ungodly Behavior from a Carnal Mindset (1 Corinthians 3:3c-4)
- Your fleshly thinking will be manifested in your life. (v3c)
- Carnal-minded Christians place men on pedestals. (v4)

DAY 3: Ministry with a Common Goal (1 Corinthians 3:5-6)
- We should be working together with the same purpose: sharing the Word of God and His Salvation. (v5a)
- We all have different talents but the same spiritual goal. (v5b)
- We are most effective when we utilize our unique spiritual gifts. (v6a)
- God gives increase to your ministry efforts when you use what He gives you for His glory. (v6b)

DAY 4: Evangelism Focus (1 Corinthians 3:7-11)
- Our ministry should be God-focused, not personality-focused. (v7)
- God-focused ministry yields dividends, harvest. (v8)
- We are God's co-workers working in unison to extend salvation to all. (v9)
- Be a kingdom-minded Christian and work heartily to promote the good news of God's saving grace. (v10a)
- Know who you are following. (v10b)
- Build your foundation on Jesus. (v11)

DAY 5: *Tilling the Heart*
Q1: How would you describe your spiritual gifts or talents?

Q2: How have your spiritual gifts/talents had an impact on the ministry of your church?
Q3: How are you using your talents in unison with other Christians to the build the Kingdom of God?
Q4: What excuses or situations are hindering you from serving in church?
Q5: Who/What are you building your spiritual foundation on?

**Flowering in the Promises of God**
"God is not unjust; he will not forget your work and the love you have shown him as you have helped his people and continue to help them." (Hebrews 6: 10)

**Morning Glory Prayer**
*Heavenly Father, there are those who are gifted with the ability to sing, others with the gift of teaching, and some you have appointed to preach the Gospel, but they all have the common goal of promoting your saving grace. God, I'm your hands and mouth used for the purpose of sharing your Gospel through the spiritual gifts and talents you gave me. I honor you with my labor of love. Today, I am available; use me as you see fit. In Jesus' name I pray, Amen.*

**Tending to the Roots**
1 Corinthians 3:1-11

**Nourishing with Praise**
Al Denson – "Be the One"
Ginny Owens – "Someone Is Searching"
Vertical Worship – "Spirit of the Living God"
Tom Inglis – "We Are One Body (Hosanna! Music)"
Twila Paris – "How Beautiful"

**Bringing in the Harvest**
Romans 12:1-2, Galatians 5:13-26, Ephesians 2:9-13, Ephesians

3:17-21, Ephesians 4:11-32, Ephesians 6:10-20, Matthew 9:37-38, 1 Corinthians 4:5, Mark 16:20

## Week 7

THE KEPT PROMISE

**Morning Glory Devotion**
"Sovereign Lord, as You have promised, you now dismiss your servant in peace. For my eyes have seen your salvation, which you have prepared in the sight of all people." (Luke 2:29-31)

**Growing in God's Word**
I opened the door to a special delivery—a bouquet of flowers of many beautiful colors! I wondered who sent me these flowers. The card attached read: *Daughter, I love you, Mom!* How did she know this was what I needed so desperately in that moment? *I hadn't said a word about what I was struggling with*, I thought with tears flowing down my face. The colors of the flowers and the message of love from my mother touched my heart and instantly removed the emptiness of depression that had been holding me emotionally paralyzed. This unexpected seed of love reminded me of the promises revealed to me through the Holy Spirit. My hope was restored and the flowers were a symbol confirming God's promise that He will bless me double for my sorrows. I will be blessed with a double portion of everlasting joy, love, and hope.

This week's Morning Glory devotion scripture about the fulfilled promise of God brought joy to my heart! Sometimes we just need confirmation and proof, just like this servant of God, a righteous and devout man who was promised through the Holy Spirit to see God's salvation before his death. Scripture says he praised God for his eyes had seen the promises.

My joy comes from knowing that, as a child of God, every unseen promise revealed to me by the Holy Spirit will come to me before my death. And just like that servant of God waiting, I too will wait for the promises of God to be manifested and that I am to be seen waiting steadfast with faith, in peace, for the manifestation of the promise revealed to me by the Holy Spirit.

**Digging Deeper into the Word** (Luke 2:22-40)

DAY 1: The Promise of a Savior (Luke 2:22-24)
- Jesus was purified according to the law of Moses. (v22)
- Jesus was anointed and consecrated to the Lord. (v23)
- A sacrifice was made for atonement in advance of his own sacrifice. (v24)

DAY 2: Salvation in the Temple (Luke 2:25-26)
- The Holy Spirit comforts us while we are in waiting. (v25)
- God preserved the righteous for the promise He made. (v26)

DAY 3: Witnessing the Promise Kept (Luke 2: 27-32)
- The Holy Spirit reveals God's promises to us. (v27-28)
- God always fulfills His promises. (v29)
- God's promise is salvation for everyone. (v30-31)
- God's promise is a savior not only for the "chosen," but for every person. (v32)

DAY 4: The Savior Revealed (Luke 2:33-40)
- Jesus was blessed and proclaimed to be the fulfillment of God's promise. (v33-34)
- His faithful servant remained in God's service for a lifetime, believing in God's promises. (v35)
- All who have seen and know bring forth corroborating evidence of the promise kept. (v36-37)
- Spread the Good News. (v38)
- Knowing their responsibility, Mary and Joseph nurtured and carefully guarded God's promise. (v39-40)

DAY 5: *Tilling the Heart*
Q1: How did you receive revelation knowledge of God's promise for you?
Q2: What do you do while in waiting for the revealed promise to be manifested?
Q3: When have you ever lost hope or had doubt while waiting for a promise?
Q4: How did you regain your hope and faith in the waiting process?
Q5: How did you feel when the revealed promise of God was fulfilled?

**Flowering in the Promises of God**
"But when he, the Spirit of truth, comes, he will guide you into all truth. He will not speak on his own; he will speak only what he hears, and he will tell you what is yet to come." (John 16:13)

**Morning Glory Prayer**
*Sovereign Lord, thank you for your promise of your Son Jesus Christ, our Redeemer, for coming into the world, and for all your spoken promises that were fulfilled in the sight for all to see. Praise your holy name! The Salvation of the Lord is here. Today, I testify to the manifestation of the promises of God in my life. In Jesus' name I pray, Amen.*

**Tending to the Roots**
Luke 2:22-40

**Nourishing with Praise**
OC Supertones – "Hold on to Jesus"
Rex Carroll – "Hands of GOD"
The Martins – "The Promise (Live)"
BeBe Winans – "He Promised Me"
Laura Story – "Faithful God"

**Bringing in the Harvest**

Luke 2:26, Luke 3:6, Luke 2:30, Leviticus 12:6, Exodus 13:12, Leviticus 5:11, Mark 15:33, Matthew 2:12, Luke 2:22, Luke 2:29, Psalms 119:166, Isaiah 9:2

# Week 8

## HE ALREADY KNOWS

**Morning Glory Devotion**
"And it shall come to pass, that before they call, I will answer; and while they are yet speaking, I will hear." (Isaiah 65:24 KJV)

**Growing in God's Word**
When you have the knowledge and understanding of the power of faith by speaking the unseen things in your life and believing you have it, it becomes your norm. Many years ago, while attending my home church, we had a special guest speaker for our Sunday Services, an Apostle from Africa.

After his powerful message, he gave an altar call invitation, during which I immediately went up for prayer. At the altar, I stood with raised hands praying as the Apostle stepped directly in front of me and said, "You will get a job promotion very soon. I let out a big shout, "I receive it!" Two years earlier, I had been applying for higher paying jobs with no success. Out of my hopelessness and frustration, I stopped submitting job applications. So, to hear this unseen promise spoken by prophecy, I was overjoyed and I believed!

The first order of business the next morning was for me to check my e-mail. The subject line of a particular e-mail that caught my attention was titled "Job Opening." Without delay, I opened the e-mail that read "Limited Applicants" had been selected for an interview to be the executive secretary for the Brigade Commander, which was a very prestigious position within my organization. I interviewed for the position and got the job!

By proclaiming, "I receive it" to the prophecy that was spoken by the Apostle connected my faith with the heart of God.

**Digging Deeper into the Word** (Isaiah 65:21-24)

DAY 1: God's Provisions for His People (Isaiah 65:21)
- God will provide a dwelling place for the chosen. (v21a)
- We will enjoy the fruits of our labor. (v21b)

DAY 2: Blessing that Endures (Isaiah 65:22)
- God can elevate you from servant to master. (v22a)
- The righteous will be blessed with long life. (v22b)
- God will provide enduring resources for His chosen people. (v22c)

DAY 3: Blessing Overflow - Generational (Isaiah 65:23-24)
- Our labor produces our prosperity. (v23a)
- The legacy of the righteous will pass down to future generations. (v23b)
- God anticipates the needs of His People (v24)
- God knows what you need before you realize what you need. (v24a)
- God answers our needs before we can even make our request known. (v24b-c)
- God's grace is at work before we can even complete our request. (v24d)
- God's love—His grace and mercies are rich and always abounding toward us. (v24e)

DAY 5: *Tilling the Heart*
Q1: How do you make your needs known to God?
Q2: What are your expectations of receiving an answer from God?
Q3: When has God met a need for you before you could even make your petitions known? How was that need met?
Q4: How did you respond to receiving God's answer?
Q5: How do you define overflow of blessing? What steps are you taking to ensure that your overflow is being passed down to your descendants?

**Flowering in the Promises of God**
"Now to him who is able to do immeasurably more than all we ask or imagine, according to his power that is at work within us." (Ephesians 3:20)

**Morning Glory Prayer**
*Heavenly Father, there's nothing new to You. Before I called, You answered; while I'm yet speaking, You heard me. Today, I affirm that your timing concerning me is perfect. In Jesus' name, I pray. Amen.*

**Tending to the Roots**
Isaiah 65:21-24

**Nourishing with Praise**
Kutless – "Need"
Laura Story – "Blessings"
Clifton Boyd – "God Already Knows"
Love & The Outcome – "The God I Know"
Sara Jordan Powell – "God Knows"

**Bringing in the Harvest**
Isaiah 55:6, Isaiah 59:1, Isaiah 30:23, Psalms 21:4, Psalms 91:15, Deuteronomy 28:3, Daniel 9:20, Daniel 10:12

# Week 9

ARE YOU ON TRACK?

**Morning Glory Devotion**
"I have swept away your offenses like a cloud, your sins like the morning mist. Return to me, for I have redeemed you." (Isaiah 44:22)

**Growing in God's Word**
For many years, because of my lack of knowledge of God's Word, I served God with the belief that you could only receive God's grace and blessings based on your good works. I stayed very busy in my church, serving others, out of duty for God because of my misunderstanding about what God expected from us. My loving Father, provided for my household regardless of my erroneous thinking. It was during my devotional time where I began to learn the biblical truths of God's word and formed an everlasting relationship with my heavenly Father.

When we seek God and desire to learn more of Him and His word, we often turn to spiritual leaders. Finding a mentor or spiritual counselor is fine, but it is equally important to study, learn, and know God's Word for yourself! If you feel yourself being led astray or getting off track, turn back to God's Word yourself. Study groups, church services, and other outside perspectives are great resources for developing your spiritual growth. However there is no substitute for learning to discern for yourself what God is communicating to you through his word.

Stay anchored in the Gospel of God's word that set you free from sin. Continue to be grounded with sound doctrine and beware of anyone who is teaching a doctrine contrary to the Word of God.

**Digging Deeper into the Word** (Isaiah 44:17-23)

DAY 1: Misguided Ways of the Backsliders (Isaiah 44:17-20)
- It is foolish to make idols of and worship anything other than God. (v17)
- False gods cannot offer salvation. (v18)
- Ignorance is costly. (v19)
- Misguided ways lead to destruction; Salvation is unattainable. (v20)

DAY 2: Ownership: God Created us for His Purpose (Isaiah 44:21)
- Remember all the things God has done for you. (v21a)
- We are His chosen people. (v21b)
- God is fully committed to us (v21c)

DAY 3: God's Forgiveness Is Endless (Isaiah 44:22)
- God removes our sins like disappearing clouds from the sky. (v22a)
- Forgiven sins are like the morning mist that is burned away by the sun. (v22b)
- Forgiveness is always extended to the backsliders. (v22c)
- He has already purchased your sins in exchange for your freedom. (v22d)

DAY 4: Homecoming Celebration (Isaiah 44:23)
- All of heaven and earth rejoices when a backslider returns.(v23a)
- The reactions of Nature: volcanos erupt and the forests dance. (v23b)
- The Redeemer is Satisfied. (v23c)
- Righteousness is restored. (v23d)

DAY 5: *Tilling the Heart*
Q1: If you have found yourself headed down a path that is leading you away from Christ, what can you do to get back on track?
Q2: What does the Bible say about how sins are forgiven and washed away forever? Do you believe that is true even if you get off track?
Q3: What does once forgiven, always forgiven mean to you?
Q4. How has your study of the Bible offered you comfort and understanding of His love and forgiveness?

Q5: If you have not been doing your own study of the Bible, what plans do you have to get back on track and learn more about Him and His Word?

## Flowering in the Promises of God
"I will cleanse them from all the sin they have committed against me and will forgive all their sins of rebellion against me." (Jeremiah 33:8)

## Morning Glory Prayer
*Heavenly Father, thank you for being a just God, blotting out and forgiving all of my sins and restoring me to your saving grace. Today, in Jesus name I declare that I am redeemed and back on track with you. In Jesus' name I pray, Amen.*

## Tending to the Roots
Isaiah 44: 21-23

## Nourishing with Praise
Casting Crowns – "If We've Ever Needed You"
Aaron Keyes and Urban – "Establish the Work of Our Hands"
Vertical Worship – "Word of God"
Casting Crowns – "Jesus, Friend of Sinners"
Anthony Evans – "Restore Me"

## Bringing in the Harvest
Acts 3:19, Psalms 51:1, Psalms 98:7, 1 Peter 1:18, Isaiah 55:7, 1 Corinthians 6:20

## Week 10

### DANGEROUS PERSUASION

**Morning Glory Devotion**
"I am confident in the Lord that you will take no other view. The one who is throwing you into confusion whoever that may be will have to pay the penalty." (Galatians 5:10)

**Growing in God's Word**
It was testimonial time at church. I stood up for the first time to share my praise report with the congregation. With all eyes and ears on me, I shared my praise report. After church, one of the older sisters approached me and said she was really excited to see me stand up to share my praise report. She gently held my hand and said she understood the joy that was in my heart and not to let negative speaking steal the victory. She continued to explain that a negative and a positive in the same sentence were contradicting and unfruitful when speaking of God's word and His mighty acts. She said, "Don't give the devil any room for praise or power."

So, I began to listen intently to others when they stood to give their testimonies so I could learn how to speak life and to exalt God. The next time I stood up to share a praise report I exalted God and exposed the Devil. The same older sister who gently instructed me when I gave my first testimonial smiled at me and said, "Your praise report honored God!"

Speak and apply God's word. Let your public acknowledgement of God's love fill the ears of the hearer with hope. Don't let doubt or disarray in your speech take away the power of God's miracles, signs, and wonders of His perfect will.

**Digging Deeper into the Word** (Galatians 5:7-13)

DAY 1: Living Up to Your Confession in Christ (Galatians 5:7-9)
- Don't get off course; apply the Word of God correctly. (v7a)
- Don't allow those with false messages to interfere with your understanding. (v7b)
- Deceitful influence is designed to turn you away from the truth of God's Word. (v8)
- One seed of doubt can multiply. (v9)

DAY 2: The Word of God Safeguards (Galatians 5:10)
- Hold strong in your faith that is grounded in God's Word. (v10a)
- False teachers will be exposed and punished. (v10b)
- Punishment extends to all falsehood inside/outside the church—anyone who intentionally teaches false doctrine. (v10c)

DAY 3: The Necessity of the Preached Gospel (Galatians 5:11)
- Paul didn't shy away from teaching the unadulterated truth of God's Word to avoid being persecuted. (v11a)
- If there wasn't sin, then the death of Jesus wouldn't have been necessary. (v11c)

DAY 4: Keep a Firm Grip on Your Liberty (Galatians 5:12-13)
- Separate yourself from false influence. (v12)
- Don't abuse your freedoms in Christ. (v13a)
- Labor in love, serve in humility with compassion and grace. (v13b)

Day 5: *Tilling the Heart*
Q1: Do you use the Bible as a reference book or as the main source for your devotional study? What other study resources do you use to enhance your spiritual growth?
Q2: How do you confirm the truth of God's Word when in doubt?
Q3: What do you see as the difference between the true interpretations of God's word versus man's opinion of God's Word?

Q4: How do you deal with a person who uses the Word of God to indulge their flesh in sin?

Q5: How confident are you that your faith is grounded in the Word of God and won't be uprooted by some other doctrine? What can you do to feel assured in that?

## Flowering in the Promises of God
"To the Jews who had believed him, Jesus said, 'If you hold to my teaching, you are really my disciples. Then you will know the truth, and the truth will set you free.'" (John 8:31-32)

## Morning Glory Prayer
*Heavenly Father, my confidence is in your Holy Word and not in man's point of view. I will not allow anyone or anything to throw me into disbelief, doubt, or confusion that will lead me to waver in my faith. Today, I will keep my trust in you, Lord, and I will run my race in faith, with perseverance and with patience for your name's sake. In Jesus' name I pray, Amen.*

## Tending to the Roots
Galatians 5:7-12

## Nourishing with Praise
Ada – "I Testify"
Amy Grant – "Thy Word"
Marvin Sapp – "My Testimony"
Eddie James – "I Exalt Thee"
Mary Mary – "I Try"

## Bringing in the Harvest
Acts 15:24, Galatians 2:2, Romans 8:28, 1 Corinthians 5:6, Philippians 3:15, Romans 9:33, Deuteronomy 23:1

## Week 11

### I'M SEALED WITH HIS PROMISE

**Morning Glory Devotion**

"And you also were included in Christ when you heard the word of truth, the gospel of your salvation. When believed, you were marked in him with a seal, the promised Holy Spirit." (Ephesians 1:13)

**Growing in God's Word**

When I said, "I do" to my Man of God, I became his wife and I inherited his surname, becoming Mrs. Yolanda Turner. On that day, I received full entitlement to and ownership of all of his assets. When I made my confession of faith and was baptized in the name of the Father, the Son and Holy Spirit, I was marked as a Child of God and sealed with all the promises of God, making me joint heirs with Christ.

Through our belief and confession of faith we are sealed with a new identity in Christ Jesus, inheriting the promise of the Holy Spirit and becoming the beneficiary of God's blessings and eternal life. Our hope is in the fact that God has guaranteed us His unchangeable promises. When we say "I do" to Jesus and accept Him as our Lord and Savior, we inherit all the promises in God, and they are Yes and Amen.

**Digging Deeper into the Word** (Ephesians 1:3-14)

DAY 1: Our Divine Blessing Comes through Christ (Ephesians 1:3-5)
- Christ is the son of God. (v3a)
- All of our spiritual blessings are in Christ. (v3b)
- We are the chosen Sons of God. (v4a)

- A Holy lifestyle is required. (v4b)
- We are made joint-heirs through Christ. (v5a)
- God created us for His purpose, not for our purpose. (v5b)

DAY 2: God's Abundance Grace (Ephesians 1:6-8)
- We must accept God's Grace. (v6a)
- We are accepted into the family of God. (v6b)
- The blood of Jesus has redeeming power. (v7a)
- Salvation comes by God's Grace. (v7b)
- God's grace is always available to us. (v8)

DAY 3: The Will of the Father Revealed in Us (Ephesians 1:9-10)
- We are enlightened by the Holy Spirit. (v9a)
- We are crafted for His purpose. (v9b)
- Heavenly authority is restored through Christ. (v10)

DAY 4: Our Inheritance Secured in Christ (Ephesians 1:11-14)
- Our promised inheritance is guaranteed through the Holy Spirit. (v11)
- We are living testimony of His greatness. (v12)
- We are God's precious treasure. (v13-14)

DAY 5: Tilling the Heart

Q1: How is God's grace reflected in your life?

Q2: How does your lifestyle reflect your Christian walk?

Q3: How would you explain how the Holy Spirit is working in your life?

Q4: What are some of your benefits as a Child of God?

Q5: What is your inheritance in Christ?

**Flowering in the Promises of God**

"For you are a people holy to the LORD your God. The LORD your God has chosen you out of all the peoples on the face of the earth to be his people, His treasured possession." (Deuteronomy 7:6)

**Morning Glory Prayer**
*Heavenly Father, when I heard the word of truth, the Gospel of my salvation, I believed! My soul is marked with your seal; I'm your child, and today the promised Holy Spirit lives in me. And I stand on your word and I declare that all promises that are in you Yes and Amen. In Jesus' name I pray, Amen.*

**Tending to the Roots**
Ephesians 1:9-14

**Nourishing with Praise**
The Williams Brothers – "What God Does"
Big Daddy Weave – "I Belong to God"
Chris Tomlin ft. Kim Walker-Smith – "First Love"
Shawn McDonald – "Closer"
Lauren Daigle – "First"

**Bringing in the Harvest**
Ephesians 2:8-10, Romans 5:17-23, Romans 8:17, 2 Corinthians 1:20-22, 2 Corinthians 5:5, John 6:27, 1 Peter 1:5, John 3:33

# Week 12

THE REWARDS OF PERSISTENT FAITH

**Morning Glory Devotion**
"And without faith it is impossible to please God, because anyone who comes to him must believe that he exists and that he
rewards those who earnestly seek him." (Hebrews 11:6)

**Growing in God's Word**
I'm alive today because of God's divine healing. At the age of
fifteen, I was diagnosed with two major diseases. They required
open-heart surgery to remove a large mass that was growing
above my heart. Because of my parents faith, God intervened
on my behalf, providing for our financial needs and ensuring
excellent medical care for me. I never saw my parents waver in
their faith and they believed fully in God's healing power. God
protected my life during my surgery and I recovered fully. It is
through this proof of His hand on my life that I can say without
a doubt that Yes! God exists

How did you come to believe that God exists? Was it a
personal experience, such as sickness, death of a loved one, or
a broken relationship? Did a friend invite you to church? Whatever the reason was for you to seek, believe, and receive God,
great is your reward of salvation and eternal life in Christ Jesus.

Your faith says, "I believe and I receive" every Word of
God. This pleases Him! Your faith will cause you to draw nearer
to God for protection, guidance, healing, provisions, and all the
desires of your heart. God will reward those who believe in faith
that all things are possible with Him.

**Digging Deeper into the Word** (Hebrews 11:1-40)

DAY 1: Unseen Faith (Hebrews 11:1-3)
- Faith is confidence in what we hope for and assurance in what we don't see. (v1)
- Our forefathers were commended for having this kind of faith. (v2)
- We understand the omnipotence of God through our faith. (v3)

DAY 2: Excellent Faith Pleases God (Hebrews 11:4-7)
- When we give our best to God, it pleases Him. (v4)
- When we believe fully in God, it pleases Him. (v5)
- When we earnestly seek God, we please Him. (v6a)
- God rewards persistent faith. (v6c)
- Faith sometimes requires us to do things that don't make sense to us or those around us. (v7a)
- Faith sometimes requires us to go without knowing where or what to expect. (v7c)

DAY 3: Committed Faith (Hebrews 11:8-16)
- When we place our faith in God, we can do the unimaginable. (v8-9)
- We can have faith because God is faithful to keep His promises. (v10)
- Promise Keeper: Inheritance passed down by Faith. (v11-12)
- Faith keeps hope alive. (v13-16)

DAY 4: Faith Hall of Famers (Hebrews 11: 17-40)
- We can look to the Bible for examples of great faith. (v17-38)
- Our biblical examples showed us what it means to keep the faith even when we believe we have been forgotten. (v39)
- God's promise through salvation is the reward for unwavering faith. (v40)

DAY 5: Tilling the Heart
Q1: What is your faith built on? How do you describe your faith?

Q2: What obstacles to your faith have you encountered in the past? What obstacles to your faith are you currently facing? What is your plan to overcome them?

Q3: What are some ways you can increase upon your faith?

Q4: What examples can you share of promises God made to you that have come to pass?

Q5: How are the Word of God, your faith, and the promises of God connected?

## Flowering in the Promises of God

"I love those who love me, and those who seek me find me." (Proverbs 8:17)

## Morning Glory Prayer

*Heavenly Father, I know you exist because of all the wonderful things you have done for me and all the impossible situations you have delivered me from. By faith, I continue to seek your righteousness and all of your promises that you have given me through your Word. Today, Lord, I thank you for all the rewards that I have received from diligently seeking you. In Jesus' name I pray, Amen.*

## Tending to the Roots

Hebrews 11:1-40

## Nourishing with Praise

Lauren Daigle – "Loyal"
Cheri Keaggy – "What Matters Most"
Kair Jobe – "Be Still My Soul (In You I Rest)"
Kirk Franklin – "He's Able"
James Fortune – "I Believe"

## Bringing in the Harvest

Matthew 11:26, Hebrews 7:19, Romans 8:24, Genesis 1:1, Genesis 4:8, John 8:51, Ezekiel 14:14, Acts 7:2, Genesis 18:9, Revelation 21:14, Hebrews 10:23, Romans 4:19

## Week 13

EXHORTATIONS

**Morning Glory Devotion**
"Keep your lives free from the love of money and be content with what you have, because God has said, 'Never will I leave you; never will I forsake you.'" (Hebrews 13:5)

**Growing in God's Word**
Money will come and money will go, but a content heart and peace in God is priceless! I had a beautiful home that I loved dearly. I really couldn't afford it on my income; but, after my divorce, I vowed to keep it, so the struggles began. My security and pride were tied up in this house. I lived in a vicious cycle of who would get paid in full and who would receive partial payments monthly for many years. An unforeseen event occurred, forcing me to sell my house and move to another state. I fought tirelessly against this move until I finally had to surrender myself to God. Breaking down in tears, I cried out for His help. His quiet, still voice spoke to my heart, *Do you trust me?* "Yes," I cried out! I clearly heard, *It's time to move forward into your new beginnings.*

I thought my contentment was in a home that actually brought me no peace of mind and only gave me a false sense of security. God set me free from this financial bondage and worry. God never left me; He always made a way. I have found true contentment in God—not in what I think I should have, but in what God has for me.

**Digging Deeper into the Word (Hebrews 13:1-8)**

DAY 1: Godly Instructions for the Believers: Godly Conduct (Hebrews 13:1-4)

- Continue serving in love. (v1)
- Be kind to everyone. (v2)
- Show empathy to the oppressed. (v3)
- Honor the sanctity of marriage. (v4)

DAY 2: Godly Instructions for the Believers: Have Faith in God (Hebrews 13:5)

- Seek the things of God. (v5a)
- Be thankful. (v5b)
- God is faithful to us. (v5c)

DAY 3: Godly Instructions for the Believers: Be Satisfied in Your Salvation (Hebrews 13:6)

- We can be confident in the confirmed promises of God. (v6a)
- He gives us strength to face our fears. (v6b)
- God's protection covers us. (v6c)

DAY 4: Godly Instructions for the Believers: Stay Grounded in the Gospel (Hebrews 13:7-8)

- Look for leaders who set a good example. (v7a)
- Follow their lead and their ways. (v7b)
- God is consistent, so what He did for them, He will do for you. (v8)

DAY 5: *Tilling the Heart*

Q1: What is your attitude towards your Christian leaders or other Christians that you serve with?

Q2: How do you treat the oppressed? How do you empathize with them?

Q3: How much time and effort do you spend on your worldly possessions? Are you satisfied with your life accomplishments?

Q4: How much do you trust God? Do you take every situation to Him in prayer?

Q5: Are you confident in your salvation? How is your relationship with God?

**Flowering in the Promises of God**
"And my God will meet all your needs according to the riches of his glory in Christ Jesus." (Philippians 4:19)

**Morning Glory Prayer**
*Heavenly Father, my state of contentment is not in my worldly possessions but in You. Today, I place my trust solely in the One who will never leave me or forsake me. Lord, my life is anchored in You. In Jesus' name I pray, Amen.*

**Tending to the Roots**
Hebrews 13:1-6

**Nourishing with Praise**
Hezekiah Walker – "Grateful"
Jekalyn Carr – "You're Bigger"
Tye Tribbett – "What Can I Do"
Byron Cage – "Broken, But I'm Healed"

**Bringing in the Harvest**
Matthew 6: 33-34, Deuteronomy 31:6, Romans 12:10, Matthew 25:35, Colossians 4:18, Galatians 5:19, Joshua 1:5, Psalms 118:6

## Week 14

BLESSED ASSURANCE

**Morning Glory Devotion**
"But Stephen, full of the Holy Spirit, looked up to heaven and saw the glory of God, and Jesus standing at the right hand of God. 'Look,' he said, 'I see heaven open and the Son of Man standing at the right hand of God.'" (Acts 7:55-56)

**Growing in God's Word**
As a young teenager, the doctors recommended that I have my tubes tied (Tubal Ligation) because of my major health issues. I was diagnosed with Myasthenia Gravis and Hyperthyroidism, and they said any future pregnancies and delivery would be a high risk for death. I had limited knowledge of God's word and promises, but I had faith and a deep love for God, so I chose to trust in God, not accepting the recommendation to have my tubes tied. I had no doubt as a young teenager that God was in Heaven and that He saw my trusting faith in Him. In the same way, Stephen saw the glory of God in his dying moments, and saw Jesus standing at the right hand of God, in Heaven. I'm a witness of God's healing power because God healed my body. I had successful pregnancies and deliveries; I'm a mother and a grandmother of beautiful children.

As believers, we should be living our lives committed to seeking and trusting in the Lord. Jesus is with us in life and in death and His comfort and loving care is never ending. My heart is settled to know that this same comfort and loving care will be with us when we die in Christ and we all will see Jesus standing at the right hand of God with open and loving arms to receive us and position us at His feet in fullness of joy and eternal life in Heaven.

**Digging Deeper into the Word** (Acts 7:1-60)

DAY 1: The History of God's Promises Proclaimed: God's Faithfulness to His People In Spite of Their Unfaithfulness to Him (Acts 7:1-54)

- History reveals God's sovereign, abundant Grace. (v1-34)
- History reveals the stubbornness of God's People. (v35-41)
- History reveals that God's people were stuck in tradition and religion—their hearts were far from Him. (v42-54)

DAY 2: Divine Comforter (Acts 7:55-56)

- The Holy Spirit emboldens and comforts us. (v55)
- Jesus stands at the right hand of God to introduce His saints to the heavenly host. (v56)

DAY 3: The Persecution and Death of a Saint (Acts 7:57-58)

- We may face evil indignation when we stand in our faith. (v57)
- Saul witnessed the murder of a saint. (v58)

DAY 4: The Love of a Saint for the Unbelievers: Bearing Witness to the Truth (Acts 7:59-60)

- In the face of adversity, pray. (v59)
- Saints pray for the forgiveness of sinners. (v60)

DAY 5: *Tilling the Heart*

Q1: What are some of God's promises that He has fulfilled for His children?

Q2: How do you act in the face of adversity?

Q3: What do you do when you are faced with adversity?

Q4: Have you ever witnessed someone passing? If so, how did you feel and what action, if any, did you take?

Q5: Have you thought about how your transition from death to life will be?

### Flowering in the Promises of God

"If you are insulted because of the name of Christ, you are bless-ed, for the Spirit of glory and of God rests on you. If you suffer, do not be ashamed, but praise God that you bear that name." (1 Peter 4:14, 16)

### Morning Glory Prayer

*Heavenly Father, I want to have a heart like Stephen, boldly sharing the gospel without fear or shame in times of adversity to the unbelievers. Today, I will continue to confess my faith until my death. In Jesus' name I pray, Amen.*

### Tending to the Roots

Acts 7:1-60

### Nourishing with Praise

Kalley Heiligenthal/We Will Not Be Shaken – "Ever Be"
The Silver Pages ft. David Leonard – "He Shouted Love"
Mia Fieldes – "Fearless"
The Brilliance – "Prayers of the People"
Christy Nockels – "My Anchor"

### Bringing in the Harvest

Genesis 33:19, Genesis 50:13, Genesis 12:6-7, Joshua 24:32, Isaiah 66:1-2, Mark 7:6-8, Mark 16:19, John 11:41, John 1:51, 1 Corinthians 10:6-10, Romans 6:1-2, Jude 4, Titus 2:11-12

# Week 15

## PEACE THAT ONLY GOD CAN GIVE

### Morning Glory Devotion

"Peace I leave with you; my peace I give you. I do not give to you as the world gives. Do not let your hearts be troubled and do not be afraid." (John 14:27)

### Growing in God's Word

There is a well-known story in the gospels of Jesus sleeping in a boat with His disciples while they were traveling to the other side of the sea. A great storm arose, frightening the disciples. Fearing for their lives, they woke Jesus from His sleep. Jesus stood up and commanded the storm to cease and said unto the sea, "Peace, be still," and the wind stopped and the sea was calm. Then Jesus asked the disciples, "Why do you have such little faith?"

When storms arise in my life and fear begins to grip me, I speak just as Jesus spoke to the storm "Peace, be still," and just as the storm obeyed Him, my storms always submit to the power of the Holy Spirit that's living in me. When faced with life's storms, with great faith, use your God-given authority in the Holy Spirit, and declare to the spirit of fear, "I'm not afraid. Get thee behind me, and Peace, Be Still, in the Name of Jesus Christ!"

Bad reports and adversity will always be part of our lives, but we no longer have to be bound with the paralyzing fear that causes our emotions to dictate our actions. With confidence, we can declare God's Word in faith, which will give us peace in our hearts and minds, eliminating all of our fears and freeing our troubled hearts. The freedom of peace allows us to con-

45

tinue trusting in God as we face all life's adversities with confidence, and to rest in the Holy Spirit that will keep our hearts and minds steadfast in Jesus, our Lord and Savior.

**Digging Deeper into the Word** (John 14:21-27)

DAY 1: Demonstration of Love (John 14:21-22)
- Love leads to obedience. (v21a)
- Submission demonstrates your love for Jesus. (v21b)
- Your love for Jesus brings God's acceptance. (v21c)
- Through faith, Christ is manifested in you. (v21d)
- Christ is manifested to the world through the love you demonstrate for others. (v22)

DAY 2: A Dwelling Place for God (John 14: 23)
- Man demonstrates his love through obedience. (v23a)
- When you commit to the word of God, He will embrace you. (v23b)
- The love of God comes into your heart when you love Him. (v23c)
- Christ lives in you. (v23d)

DAY 3: Denying Salvation (John 14:24-25)
- Those who do not love Jesus deny Him. (v24a-b)
- Jesus knows He will be rejected by many. (v25)

DAY 4: Demonstration of the Holy Spirit: Power of Peace (John 14:26-27)
- The Holy Spirit is your advocate. (v26a)
- The Holy Spirit is a reminder of the gift of salvation. (v26b)
- The Holy Spirit teaches you in the Word of God, bringing understanding and wisdom. (v26d)
- Peace comes through the Holy Spirit. (v27a)
- Peace empowers you. (v27b)
- The peace from the Holy Spirit surpass all understanding. (27c)
- There is no fear in Jesus. (v27d)

DAY 5: *Tilling the Heart*
Q1: How does your peace demonstrate Christ's love?
Q2: How does the Word of God bring you peace?
Q3: How would you describe the Holy Spirit? Does He dwell in you?
Q4: What verse(s) of scripture do yo turn to for peace when you are afraid or troubled?
Q5: What peace have you found in the Holy Spirit? How has the power of peace empowered you?

## Flowering in the Promises of God
"And the peace of God, which transcends all understanding, will guard your hearts and your minds in Christ Jesus." (Philippians 4:7)

## Morning Glory Prayer
*Heavenly Father, my ears are filled with the confusion of this world and my eyes are consumed with the works of evildoers. Today, I declare peace as you give it–your peace that comforts my troubled heart and overshadows my fears. I will trust you and not be afraid. In Jesus' name, I pray. Amen.*

## Tending to the Roots
John 14:23-27

## Nourishing with Praise
Vanessa Bell Armstrong – "Peace, Be Still"
Marvin Sapp – "Perfect Peace"
Yolanda Adams – "Be Still"
Darlene Zschech – "In Jesus' Name"
Chris Tomlin – "Whom Shall I Fear (God of Angel Armies) "

## Bringing in the Harvest
1 Corinthians 6:19-20, Colossians 3:4, Romans 8:10-11, Matthew 8:24-27, Matthew 14:22-33, Mark 4:35-41, Proverbs 4:23, John 14:1, John 16:33, Isaiah 26:3

# Week 16

## THE BLESSING IS IN THE INSTRUCTIONS

### Morning Glory Devotion

"I will instruct you and teach you in the way you should go; I will counsel you with my loving eye on you." (Psalms 32:8)

### Growing in God's Word

For years I covered my shame under layers of clothing to hide the burns I suffered in domestic abuse. In my mind, I was an ugly, scared burn victim. While in the hospital recovering from second and third degree burns, I demanded that the hospital staff cover every mirror that I had to pass in my room. I couldn't bear the thought of seeing myself; but, with encouragement from my mother, I was able to look into the mirror before my release from the hospital. I wore clothing that hid my scars for many years. In God's loving pursuit of me, he removed the distractions of the world and awakened my desire to have an authentic relationship with Him. I was able to submit myself to God, and through that submission, God was able to expose all the obstacles that kept us apart. Through my personal devotion time and diligently seeking God I learned the heart of God, I was able to release shame and low self-esteem. I received revelation knowledge in God's Word that says I'm fearfully and wonderfully made. God's love and watchful eye protected and kept me safe. Take time to communicate with God, learn the mind of God, His heart, and His will for your life. Pray, read the Bible, meditate, worship, seek spiritual direction, and obey God's instruction, for it is life-saving and will protect you from all hidden dangers. Our Heavenly Father is attentive to all our comings and goings.

**Digging Deeper into the Word** (Psalms 32:1-11)

Day 1: The Blessing of God's Forgiveness (Psalms 32:1-5)
- God's forgiveness gives us a clean conscience before God. (v1)
- God's forgiveness removes the stain of sin. (v2a)
- Confessing our sin frees our soul from burdens. (Psalms 32:3-5)

Day 2: The Blessing of God's Protection (Psalms 32:6-7)
- Diligently seek God in prayer. (v6a)
- No harm comes to those who continue seeking Him. (v6b)
- God shields us. (v7a)
- God preserves us in our troubles and His deliverance surrounds us. (v7b)

Day 3: The Benefits of God's Instructions (Psalms 32:8-9)
- God promises to instruct and teach us with His Word. (v8a)
- God will always guide us and never leave us. (v8b)
- Don't be the self-willed person who lacks understanding. (v9a)
- Don't be the self-willed person who lacks control. (v9b)

Day 4: Submitting to Godly Counsels Leads to Joy (Psalms 32:10-11)
- Rebellion leads to sorrows. (v10a)
- Those who trust God receive His unfailing love (v10b)
- Rejoice in the Lord; you are free from your sins. (v11)

DAY 5: *Tilling the Heart*

Q1: How do you know you are forgiven? How are you operating in the gift of the Holy Spirit?

Q2: How diligent are you in seeking God's guidance? Are you living under God's protection?

Q3: In what ways are you listening and following God's instructions as you pursue His will for your life?

Q4: When have you found yourself in a situation where you rebelled against God's counsel? What were the results of that decision?

Q5: How has your submission to Christ brought you joy?

**Flowering in the Promises of God**
"For this God is our God forever and ever; He will be our guide even to the end." (Psalms 48:14)

**Morning Glory Prayer**
*Heavenly Father, give me a teachable spirit; instruct me in the ways I should go. Continue to counsel and watch over me. Today, I open my ears and my heart to hear and obey. Order my steps as I move according to your purpose. In Jesus' name I pray, Amen.*

**Tending to the Roots**
Psalms 32:8-11

**Nourishing with Praise**
Nicole Nordeman – "Finally Free"
Kurt Carr – "God Blocked It"
Tramaine Hawkins – "Trust and Obey"
Elevation Worship – "I Have Decided"
CeCe Winans – "I Surrender ALL"

**Bringing in the Harvest**
Psalms 51:13, 2 Peter 1:5-7, Psalms 25:8, Psalms 33:18, Psalms 34:11, Psalms 73:24, Psalms 143:8

# Week 17

## FLOURISHING IN YOUR SPIRITUAL GROWTH

### Morning Glory Devotion

"For this very reason, make every effort to add to your faith goodness; and to goodness, knowledge; and to knowledge, self-control; and to self-control, perseverance; and to perseverance, godliness, and to godliness, mutual affection; and to mutual affection, love." (2 Peter 1:5-7)

### Growing in God's Word

In our Christian walk, there are many levels of growth and valuable lessons to learn through them. It's just like the growth and learning process for a toddler. He learns to stand, walk, talk, dress, and feed himself. He is taught how to be safe and to avoid danger. He learns the values and rules of life—how to live according to the law and have integrity and respect for all mankind.

Every morning, as my children walked out the door to catch the school bus, I would wish them a good day, saying, "Make good choices." They understood the value of making good choices and accepting the consequences for their choices. They knew they would be held accountable for their actions. We always shared dinner together at the table, and our conversation usually started when I called on each child by name. One evening at dinnertime, I called Ebony's name and asked, "Did you make good choices today?" "Well, mom," she replied, "I almost made a bad choice today, but I could hear you in my head saying, 'Make good choices, or be ready to deal with the consequences of your actions,'" and then, with a big smile, Ebony proudly announced, "I made a good choice, I had a good day!"

As believers, we learn by the renewal of our minds and being transformed and purified by the grace of the Holy Spirit. We grow in knowledge of the purpose and will of God. We learn to resist worldly temptations and traps set up to cause us to sin. We grow stronger through patience in times of tribulation. We learn the heart of God through seeking him, praying, listening, and studying the Word of God diligently. We stay in relationship with God by obeying his commandments. And our spiritual growth will produce godly character of love and kindness toward all. A growing Christian bears much fruit.

**Digging Deeper into the Word** (2 Peter 1:1-9)

DAY 1: Precious Gift of Faith Obtained through Righteousness (2 Peter 1:1-3)
- We obtain the righteousness of God through Salvation. (v1)
- We obtain the abundance of grace and peace through the knowledge of Christ. (v2)
- God's Divine Power provides power to live a godly life, which we obtain through knowledge of Christ. (v3a)
- God's righteousness calls us into faith and grants us the necessities of life through the knowledge of Christ. (v3c)

DAY 2: Advocate for Spiritual Growth (2 Peter 1:4)
- God gives us Divine Promises. (v4a)
- Through those promises we partake of the divine nature of God. (v4b)
- We commune with God when we escape the lust of the world. (4c)

DAY 3: Supplementing Your Faith (2 Peter 1:5-7)
- As Christians, we are called to diligently seek to grow our faith and support the faith of others. (v5a-c)
- We are called to increase our virtue with knowledge of Christ. (v5d)
- We are called to increase our knowledge with self-control. (v6a)

- We are called to increase our self-control with faithfulness. (v6b)
- We are called to increase our faithfulness with godly living. (v6c)
- We are called to increase our godly living with kindness. (v7a)
- We are called to increase our kindness with the love of Christ. (v7b)

DAY 4: Faith Supplements Increases Spiritual Growth (2 Peter 1:8-9)
- As we increase, we will flourish in our faith and be more effective and productive in our Christian lives. (v8)
- Lacking these characteristics causes us to be blind and remain in bondage to our sin. (v9)

DAY 5: *Tilling the Heart*
Q1: How have adversities and victories in life helped you to grow spiritually?
Q2: What are the noticeable changes you see in your spiritual growth?
Q3: How are you bearing fruit in your Christian walk?
Q4: In what areas in your life do you need less of you and more of God?
Q5: How has this devotional study helped you to identify your spiritual growth?

## Flowering in the Promises of God

"The righteous flourish like a palm tree, they will grow like a cedar of Lebanon; planted in the house of the LORD, they will flourish in the courts of our God. They still bear fruit in old age; they will stay fresh and green, proclaiming the LORD is upright; he is my Rock, and there is no wickedness in him." (Psalms 92:12-15)

**Morning Glory Prayer**

*Heavenly Father, help me to not become complacent in my spiritual growth. Teach me your attributes and nurture them in me. Mature me through your knowledge and grace. Increase my faith and let the fruits of the spirit flourish in me. Let the evidences of my spiritual growth be seen in my lifestyle, and today and every day, may your Holy Spirit produce kindness and love in me toward my fellow man. In Jesus' name I pray, Amen.*

**Tending to the Roots**
2 Peter 1:1-9

**Nourishing with Praise**
William Murphy – "It's Working"
Malcolm Williams – "Increase My Faith"
Donald Lawrence & The Tri-City Singers – "Bless Me (Prayer of Jabez)"
Yunek – "Got Fruit"
Donald Lawerence – "Spiritual"

**Bringing in the Harvest**
Colossians 1:9-11, Colossians 2:3, Luke 21:19, Romans 12:10, 1 Peter 2:2-3, 2 Timothy 2:15, Ephesians 3:14-19, Ephesians 4:14-15

# Week 18

## COMING BACK ANEW!

**Morning Glory Devotion**
"So from now on we regard no one from a worldly point of view. Though we once regarded Christ in this way, we do so no longer. Therefore, if anyone is in Christ, the new creation has come; The old has gone, the new is here!" (2 Corinthians 5:16-17)

**Growing in God's Word**
In the past, I based my self-worth on worldly beliefs of what success and beauty should look like. All I could see was an abused woman who had two failed marriages, living barely above the poverty line—a single parent with two daughters who had been abandoned. All of my brokenness caused me to be blinded to God's grace, leaving me with disbelief of God's Word concerning me.

As a Christian, I would encourage others with the Word of God and all His promises concerning them. However, I lacked faith in the very promises I was encouraging others to have. But God! He saw my heart's desire to trust and to learn of Him. I desired to have all the promises of God for myself as well as for others.

The more I desired of God, the more I sought after Him through prayer and the study of His Word. The more I studied and prayed, the more the Holy Spirit exposed my brokenness. He transformed my thinking of self-defeat that held me captive. He cultivated my heart and removed the contaminated ground with new living soil, His "Word of life" giving me a new heart. He planted the seeds of truth in my mind and nurtured it with his Agape Love and revealed to my Spirit that I am fearfully and wonderfully made in Him. I'm the apple of His eye. I'm more valuable than rubies. God's love took root in my heart through His Word. I understood the true meaning of beauty. God isn't a religious figure; he is my Heavenly Father who created me in His beautiful image and made me righteous in Him and justified me by His saving grace. God renewed my heart and my thinking. My character, conduct, and principles are all anew. I'm God's work-manship created for His works, I'm a new creation reconciled through the redemption of Jesus Christ, the Son of God.

**Digging Deeper into the Word** (2 Corinthians 5:15-21)

DAY 1: New Identity in Christ: Name Change (2 Corinthians 5:15-16)
- Our lives are no longer ours; we belong to Christ. (v15)
- We have a new spiritual identity through Christ (v16)

DAY 2: New Life in Christ (2 Corinthians 5:17)
- We are covered by the blood of Christ. (v17a)
- We have a new spiritual nature in Christ. (v17b)
- The bondage of our sin nature is broken. (v17c)
- We have power over sin through Jesus. (v17d)

DAY 3: God's Reconciliation Plan (2 Corinthians 5:18-19)
- Reconciliation is made possible by Jesus' death on the cross. (v18a)
- Our ministry of reconciliation is to spread the Gospel, restoring humanity back to its righteous habitation. (v18c)
- Jesus' atonement for our sins reconciles us to God. (v19)

DAY 4: Ambassadors of Christ (2 Corinthians 5:20-21)
- We are chosen representatives of Jesus. (v20a)
- Our mission is to share the message of reconciliation with others. (v20b)
- Christ Jesus took on our sins. (v21a)
- We are made righteous through our Savior, Jesus Christ. (v21b)

DAY 5: *Tilling the Heart*

Q1: How would you explain the biblical meaning of reconciliation?

Q2: How did you get delivered from your sin nature?

Q3: Have you ever gone back to your old sin nature? If so, why?

Q4: As a born again Christian, did you receive a new nature? If so, what changes in your life can you attribute to your new nature?

Q5: How do you see yourself as a child of God? Do you have power over sin? If so, can you describe how you have been empowered?

## Flowering in the Promises of God

"For we are God's handiwork, created in Christ Jesus to do good works, which God prepared in advance for us to do." (Ephesians 2:10)

## Morning Glory Prayer

*Heavenly Father, I have been reconciled back to you through your Son, Christ Jesus, who knew no sin; and, because I have accepted Him as my Lord and Savior, I am a new person with new principles and character that has put my past sins behind me. Today, I celebrate liberty in Christ and your grace that covers my life and my new beginnings in you. I am redeemed! In Jesus' name I pray, Amen.*

## Tending to the Roots

2 Corinthians 5:15-21

## Nourishing with Praise

VaShawn Mitchell – "Joy"

Crystal Lewis – "Beauty for Ashes"

JJ Weeks Band – "Let Them See You"

Travis Greene – "You Waited"

Lara Martin – "God Sees You"

## Bringing in the Harvest
Philippians 3:4, Isaiah 43:18, Isaiah 65:17, Colossians 1:20, Colossians 1:22, Romans 5:10, Romans 3:25

## Week 19

ALWAYS ACKNOWLEDGING GOD

**Morning Glory Devotion**

"Are not five sparrows sold for two pennies? Yet not one of them is forgotten by God. Indeed, the very hairs of your head are all numbered. Don't be afraid; you are worth more than many sparrows. 'I tell you, whoever acknowledges me before others, the Son of Man will also acknowledge before the angels of God.'" (Luke 12:6-8)

**Growing in God's Word**

Praise God for godly relationships with our sisters and brothers in Christ who speak biblical truths and hold us accountable based on God's Word. My best friend Lora was that person for me. She would call me and say, "God put you on my heart today," and immediately she would begin to speak God's words of life over me, "God hears you. Don't be discouraged and don't give up. Your breakthrough is coming, you are an overcomer. Don't settle for less, God has the best for you. God's perfect plan concerning you is worth waiting for, keep trusting in God." And then she would pray for me. Her prayers and words of encouragement strengthened my stance while in waiting for the promises of God. I was able to re-direct my focus on God's words and not on man's views. I continue to encourage myself by confessing out loud God's words over my life. She was right about it all— not to give up, to wait and not to settle. God blessed me with His very best!

There is nothing hidden or concealed from God—our heart, our thoughts, and our motives are known to Him. As Christians, we must always hold reverence for God in our actions, in our words, and in our service to Him. Reverence not only means to *fear God;* but, it also means to live a lifestyle in obedience to God's Word and to His purposes for our lives. Let your confession of love and acknowledgement for Christ Jesus be your safeguard from hidden agendas, weariness, and deceit. You are very valuable to God; He knows the exact number of hairs on your head; God cares for the smallest things with great interest and He cares intensely for you. You are His precious child, and when you find yourself standing before man's judgment and destructive devices, remember that God has given you the Holy Spirit for your protection and defense. So, whatever pressures you may be facing in your Christian walk and service for God, don't let it cause you to stop acknowledging God.

**Digging Deeper into the Word** (Luke 12:1-12)

DAY 1: Instructions on Christian Leadership: Hypocrisy Exposed (Luke 12:1)
- We must be on guard against those who pretend to be righteous. (v1a)
- There are many who are hypocrites. (v1b)

DAY 2: Revealing of the Heart (Luke 12:2-3)
- God knows and sees all things. (v2a)
- Deceit will be exposed. (v2b)
- Secret conversations will be exposed publicly. (v3)

DAY 3: Reverence for God (Luke 12:4-7)
- Jesus warned us not to be afraid of man who has no authority over our souls. (v4)
- Instead we should fear him who has authority to condemn us to eternal damnation. (v5)
- God does not forget those who acknowledge Him. (v6)
- God cherishes those who revere Him. (v7)

DAY 4: Proclamation of Jesus as your Lord and Savior (Luke 12:8-12)

- Jesus stands before God on behalf of those who acknowledge Him. (v8b)
- He will not advocate on Judgment Day for those who have denied Him. (v9)
- Those who give in to the pressure of men can be forgiven. (v10a)
- Denial of the existence of God will be condemned. (v10b)
- Have confidence in God when you are being judged by men. (v11)
- The Holy Spirit is your defense lawyer. (v12)

DAY 5: *Tilling the Heart*

Q1: Have you ever publicly confessed that Jesus is your Lord and Savior? If not, are you willing today to confess that Christ has died for your sins and that you are willing to follow His plan for your life?

Q2: What does it mean to make Jesus your Lord and Savior?

Q3: When have you been ashamed to publicly acknowledge Christ or that you are a Christian?

Q4: Has anyone ever questioned your Christianity? If so, how did you respond?

Q5: Have you ever felt the need to step down from serving in the church or have you walked away from a church because of an untrustworthy Christian leader? How did you resolve that issue? In what ways have you continued serving God?

## Flowering in the Promises of God

"Whoever has the Son has life; whoever does not have the Son of God does not have life." (1 John 5:12)

## Morning Glory Prayer

*Heavenly Father, I'm precious in your sight and you know the very number of hairs on my head. I'm valuable to you. I'm your beloved child and you call me by name before the angels in Heaven. Today, I acknowledge you before men and confess that Jesus Christ is the Son of God. In Jesus' name I pray, Amen.*

**Tending to the Roots**
Luke 12:1-12

**Nourishing with Praise**
Big Tent Revival – "If Loving God Was a Crime"
Carman – "We Are Not Ashamed"
William Murphy – "Praying for You"
Nathaniel Bassey ft. Micah Stampley – "This God is Too Good"
Kirk Franklin – "The Lamb of God"

**Bringing in the Harvest**
Romans 10:9-11, Mark 8:15, Mark 4:22, Matthew 10:27-29, Luke 9:26

# Week 20

## DECLARED RIGHTEOUS!

**Morning Glory Devotion**
"However, to the one who does not work but trusts God who justifies the ungodly, their faith is credited as righteousness. Da-vid says the same thing when he speaks of the blessedness of the one to whom God credits righteousness apart from works: 'Blessed are those whose transgressions are forgiven, whose sins are covered. Blessed is the one whose sin the Lord will nev-er count against them.' " (Romans 4:5-8)

**Growing in God's Word**
I was that person who worked multiple auxiliaries and volun-teered for special projects within the church without ceasing. I wanted God to know that I was about His business; and surely He would take care of my affairs and bless me, but my thinking and my heart did not line up with God's Word! My works were performed out of duty and provided distractions from my bro-kenness. My works unto God were dead work!

What God truly desires is a personal relationship, not hands that are too busy to spend time with Him. When I got tired of being tired physically and spiritually, that's when I totally surrendered myself to God. The Holy Spirit revealed to my heart that I didn't have to work for God's love or approval to receive His promises of blessings concerning me. God reciprocates with blessings and promises that He gives without requiring any works from us, He only requires our faith and love. Our Salvation is the "gift" of eternal life that was paid by our Lord and Savior.

**Digging Deeper into the Word** (Romans 4:1-16)

DAY 1: Justified by Faith (Romans 4:1-3)
- Like Abraham, we should act on our faith and in obedience to God's command. (v1)
- We are not justified by our works before God. (v2)
- Only faith is credited as righteousness. (v3)

DAY 2: Righteousness credited by Faith (Romans 4:4-6)
- Wages are an obligation, not a gift, for those who work. (v4)
- For those who do not work, it is their faith that brings them righteousness. (v5)
- Righteousness is considered apart from works. (v6)

DAY 3: Blessedness of Forgiveness (Romans 4:7-8)
- Those whose transgressions are forgiven are blessed. (v7a)
- Their transgressions are covered by the blood of Christ. (v7b)
- Blessed are those whose sin the Lord will never count against them. (v8)

DAY 4: Sealed in Faith (Romans 4:9-16)
- We are not righteous because we follow man's laws and customs. (v9-10)
- Righteousness is sealed by faith. (v11)
- The righteous follow Abraham's example of faith. (v12)
- Our righteousness comes by faith. (v13)
- Righteousness is cancelled out by man's laws and customs. (v14-15)
- We will receive the promise of righteousness through grace and faith. (v16)

DAY 5: *Tilling the Heart*
Q1: How does your faith justify your salvation?
Q2: What does receiving salvation as a gift from God mean to you?
Q3: What part do you think your works play in receiving God's

love and forgiveness?

Q4: How do you feel your confession in Christ has justified you in God's eyes?

Q5: How do you explain righteousness to an unbeliever?

## Flowering in the Promises of God

"For it is with your heart that you believe and are justified, and it is with your mouth that you confess and are saved." (Romans 10:10)

## Morning Glory Prayer

*Heavenly Father, my confession of faith has made me righteous through Christ. Lord, thank you for freeing me from the bond-age of works, and gifting me with faith in your promises. It's my desire to grow stronger in my faith and relationship with you. In Jesus' name I pray, Amen.*

## Tending to the Roots

Romans 4:1-16

## Nourishing with Praise

Mathussain – "Gift of Love"

Ashes Remain – "On My Own"

Lou Gramm Band – "You Saved Me"

Smokie Norful – "Justified"

## Bringing in the Harvest

Romans 3:5, 1 Corinthians 1:31, James 2:23, John 6:29, James 2:18, Psalms 32:1, John 3:33, Romans 3:30

## Week 21

### THE GLORY OF GOD

**Morning Glory Devotion**
"May these words of my mouth and this meditation of my heart be pleasing in your sight, LORD, my Rock and my Redeemer." (Psalms 19:14)

**Growing in God's Word**
I have cried many tears, but not all of them are tears of anguish. There are times my heart overflows with deep gratitude and admiration, and through those tears my worship is expressed with the unspeakable joy that I have for God.

When I think of all of His goodness shown toward me, my joy spills over. He has delivered me from destruction, sacrificing His life so that I may have eternal life. Great is His name; Jehovah (My Lord), Jehovah-Jireh (My Provider), Jehovah-Rapha (My Healer), Jehovah-Nissi (My Banner), Jehovah-Shalom (My Peace), Jehovah-Tsori (My Strength) and Jehovah-El Shaddai (Almighty God). I proclaim you are my first love and all that's within me will praise you!

If you are struggling with fear, anxiety, sadness, or other difficulties, start praising God. You will find your mind is shifted away from those feelings and you can begin to see the hope that God offers you.

**Digging Deeper into the Word** (Psalms 19:1-14)

DAY 1: God's Glory Revealed (Psalms 19:1-3)
- Heaven declares God's Glory. (v1a)
- The firmaments portray the works of His hands. (v1b)
- Day and night proclaim His knowledge. (v2)

- All of creation offers praises to the Creator from within (v3)

DAY 2: The Revealing Light (Psalms 19:4-6)
- God's Word reveals all things like the brightness of a rising sun. (v4)
- Nothing is hidden from the brightness of the sun. (v6)

DAY 3: The Word of God: Protector of the Soul (Psalms 19:7-11)
- The wisdom of God's Word is perfect and trustworthy. (v7)
- The Word of God brings joy to the heart and enlightens the mind. (v8)
- The enduring Word of God is just and righteous. (v9)
- The Word of God is sweeter than honeycomb to those who taste it. (v10)
- There are rewards for the keeper of God's Word. (v11)

DAY 4: Prayers of a Righteous Man (Psalms 19:12-14)
- Ask God to unmask your faults. (v12)
- Ask God to keep you from your desire to sin. (v13a)
- Let us not be defenseless against our sins. (v13b)
- Ask God to reveal the condition of your heart, thoughts, and motives. (v14)

DAY 5: *Tilling the Heart*
Q1: How do you declare God's glory?
Q2: How has God's Word brought joy to your heart and enlightened your mind?
Q3: What warnings have you received through the Holy Spirit when you were in a sinful state? Did you take heed?
Q4: What sin(s) have been revealed to you as presumptuous sin—sins committed in ignorance?
Q5: What sin(s) have you deliberately committed, and why?

**Flowering in the Promises of God**
"Now the Lord is the Spirit, and where the Spirit of the Lord is, there is freedom. And we all, who with unveiled faces contem-

plate the Lord's glory, are being transformed into his image with ever-increasing glory, which comes from the Lord, who is the Spirit." (2 Corinthians 3:17-18)

## Morning Glory Prayer

*Heavenly Father, may the words of my mouth be sweet to your ears. Let the meditation of my heart touch your heart. Let my representation of you be acceptable in your sight. O Lord, forgive me of my hidden faults. Cleanse me of anything that's not like you, and let my worship and praise be pleasing unto you. Today, I sing to thee. In Jesus' name I pray, Amen.*

## Tending to the Roots
Psalms 19:1-14

## Nourishing with Praise
David Crowder Band – "You Never Let Go"
Jason Denison – "Names of God"
Aaron Shust – "Never Been a Greater Love"
Tasha Cobbs Leonard – "The Name of Our God"

## Bringing in the Harvest
Psalms 119:127, Psalms 119:142, Proverbs 8:11, Psalms 58:11, Psalms 139:24, Ezekiel 45:20, Psalms 119:133, Isaiah 47:4, Deuteronomy 18:13

# Week 22

## SALVATION THROUGH THE CONFESSION OF YOUR FAITH

**Morning Glory Devotion**
"If you declare with your mouth, 'Jesus is Lord,' and believe in your heart that God raised him from the dead, you will be saved. For it is with your heart that you believe and are justified, and it is with your mouth that you profess your faith and are saved." (Romans 10:9-10)

**Growing in God's Word**
The evidence of God in my life is displayed in my daily walk. When I accepted Christ Jesus as my Lord and Savior and was baptized in His name, I took on God's attributes. One day a co-worker approached me and asked, "You are a Christian, right?" I responded that I was. "I knew it," she said with excitement! She began to identify my good works that represented Christ to her and continued by saying, "I've been watching you and I notice that everyone you come into contact with, you greet with kindness. I've never heard a negative or filthy word come out of your mouth. I see all the positive quotes that you have on your desk. I have walked into the break room and witnessed you praying with others. Every morning, when I walk through the office door, your face always greets me with a smile that seems to never disappear. When I'm having a bad day it's your smile that reminds me that there is a light at the end of the tunnel." She then said, "I want what you have!"

I quickly responded, "You can have it today!" I was overjoyed while praising God in my heart. I explained to her that my joy and peace comes from trusting and loving Christ Jesus. I've learned to place all of my hope and happiness in GOD, not in man or worldly possessions. I'm not perfect, but I believe in a Perfect God. I shared the Gospel with her and she rededicated her life back to Christ Jesus.

As a Christian, our service to the Lord is rewarded. If we live out our confession of faith in Christ Jesus through our living, others will be drawn unto Him. We as believers are to share the gospel of Christ with those who don't know of Him; but, it is Jesus, our Redeemer, who saves the unbeliever and restores the backslider. Only the Redeemer can transform our hearts and minds, giving us perfect peace and everlasting joy.

**Digging Deeper into the Word** (Romans 10:1-13)

DAY 1: God's Chosen People Fail to Accept Salvation (Romans 10:1-4)
- As Christians, our deepest desire should be to see others saved. (v1)
- Many may have a zeal for God that doesn't line up with the truth of God's Word. (v2)
- Many seek to create their own righteousness based on works. (v3)
- Christ fulfilled the law to bring righteousness to all who believe by faith. (v4a)
- Righteousness cannot be obtained through man's efforts of how well they keep the law; rather, it must be obtained through Christ by faith. (v4b)

DAY 2: Obtaining Righteousness: Works vs. Faith (Romans 10:5-7)
- The Old Testament Covenant was based on obedience to the Law. Man is incapable of doing everything that the Law requires, and the law had no means to obtain righteousness except through efforts. (v5)
- The New Testament Covenant brought righteousness through Christ by Faith. Christ succeeded where the Old Testament Covenant failed. (v6a)
- God chose Israel and made them His people, not because of their righteousness. (v6b-7)

DAY 3: Christ and the Gospel: The Preaching of the Word of God Through the Gospel, Faith Is Easy to Obtain (Romans 10:8-10)

- The gospel teaches that righteousness through faith is near you; it's not hidden. (v8)
- Righteousness is available through confession of faith. (v9a)
- Believe in the death, burial, and resurrection and confess Jesus is Lord. (v9b)
- Out of the overflow of the heart, the month confesses. (v10)

DAY 4: Salvation Is Open to Everyone (Romans 10:11-13)

- Salvation is for everyone. (v11)
- God does not play favorites. (12)
- All who call on Him will be saved. (v13)

DAY 5: *Tilling the Heart*

Q1: What are you doing to help others find salvation?

Q2: How does your level of zeal for helping others find faith line up with God's Word and truth on salvation.

Q3: How would you explain God's righteousness to an unbeliever?

Q4: What does being saved in Christ mean to you?

Q5: What would you say to an unbeliever who asks why you are saved?

**Flowering in the Promises of God**

"Whoever acknowledges me before others, I will also acknowledge before my Father in heaven." (Matthew 10:32)

**Morning Glory Prayer**

*Heavenly Father, I declare that Jesus is Lord. I believe He has risen from the dead and that I'm saved. Because of my belief and my declaration of faith, I am righteous! In Jesus' name I pray, Amen.*

**Tending to the Roots**
Romans 10:1-13

**Nourishing with Praise**
Scott Bacher – "Salvation Is Born – Sovereign Grace"
Elevation – "Give Me Faith (Acoustic)"
Hillsong United – "I Belong to You"
Michael W. Smith – "Breathe"
Chris Tomlin – "I Lift My Hands"

**Bringing in the Harvest**
Nehemiah 9:29, Deuteronomy 30:4,12-14, Hebrews 13:20, Luke 12:8, Romans 10:9, Isaiah 28:16, Romans 9:33, Leviticus 18:5, Isaiah 28:16, Isaiah 52:7, Isaiah 53: 1, Joel 2:32

# Week 23

## THE LORD, MY KEEPER

**Morning Glory Devotion**
"The Lord will keep you from all harm—he will watch over your life. The Lord shall preserve your going out and your coming in from this time forth, and even forevermore." (Psalms 121:7-8 NKJV)

**Growing in God's Word**
I was driving home from work on a very cold day. Having grown up in California, I was not familiar with "black ice" or what it does to the roadways. While driving I was listening to the gospel song "Goin' Up Yonder." I approached a one-lane bridge that stood approximately three stories high and I did not know the lane was completely covered with a thin coating of black ice. I lost control of my car, fishtailing from side to side, and ended up headed down the opposite direction. I fought with all my strength to regain control of my car, but the more I fought, the more it worsened.

As I continued to fight to regain control of the car, I screamed out, "GOD HELP ME!" My call for help was answered with a repeated question from the Holy Spirit, *Do you trust me? Do you trust me?* I screamed out, "YES, help me!" I heard a calm voice commanding me to *Let Go* of the steering wheel. In terror, I heard myself saying, "If I let go, I will die." Again, the calm voice of the Holy Spirit spoke *Let Go*. Out of exhaustion, I cried out to God, "Please, keep me!" I looked up to Heaven and I let go. My car did a complete spinout and landed on top of the bridge railing making a motionless stop!

My life had been protected and saved by God! God knew the danger that I would face that day before I did, and He protected me from all harm and danger. That day, His divine presence was revealed to me. God is always with me, watching over my goings and my comings, providing a safe haven for me in every aspect of my daily life.

**Digging Deeper into the Word** (Psalms 121:1-8)

DAY 1: The Keeper of Our Soul (Psalms 121: 1-2)
- Look to the Creator who provides your help. (v1)
- Acknowledge the Creator who provides our help. (v2)

DAY 2: The Observant One: Attentive to All Our Needs (Psalms 121: 3-4)
- God strengthens us so we don't slip in our faith and our walk with Him. (v3a)
- God, the watchful keeper, always guides our lives and directs our pathways. (v3b)
- God is always available to His chosen people. (v4)

DAY 3: The Guardian (Psalms 121: 5-6)
- We stand in the shadows of God's strength, living under His protection. (v5)
- God overrides the sun and the moon (everything in creation) to protect us. (v6)

DAY 4: God's Preservation (Psalms 121:7-8)
- God keeps us from being overtaken by the evil of sin. (v7a)
- God is the keeper of our soul. (7b)
- God provides a safe haven and keeps us safe in every aspect of our daily lives. (v8a)
- God provides protection all the days of our lives and into eternity. (v8b)

DAY 5: *Tilling the Heart*
Q1: Who do you call on when you are in a dangerous situation?
Q2: What dangerous situation h as G od delivered you from? How?
Q3: How does God preserve you from evil?
Q4: Who do you turn to when you are desperately in need?
Q5: What does it mean, "He will keep your soul?"

## Flowering in the Promises of God
"Blessed shall you be when you come in, and blessed shall you be when you go out." (Deuteronomy 28:6 NKJV)

## Morning Glory Prayer
*Heavenly Father, you are the keeper of all things. Thank you for your promises to preserve me from evil. Father, I place all my confidence i n y ou only. I w ill stay u nder y our protective care. You are the watchful keeper over my going out and my coming in today and forevermore. In Jesus' name I pray, Amen.*

## Tending to the Roots
Psalms 121:1-8

## Nourishing with Praise
Fred Hammond – "No Weapon"
Donnie McClurkin – "Great Is Your Mercy"
Carrie Underwood – "Jesus, Take the Wheel"
Sinach – "Way Maker"

## Bringing in the Harvest
Isaiah 40:26, Psalms 124:8, Isaiah 27:3, Isaiah 25:4, Psalms 91:10, Psalms 115:18, Matthew 10:28, Genesis 1:16

# Week 24

## JESUS: GOD IN THE FLESH

### Morning Glory Devotion

"In the beginning was the Word, and the Word was with God, and the Word was God. He was with God, in the beginning." (John 1:1-2)

### Growing in God's Word

Early in my Christian life, I didn't always walk in the light and the liberty, which Christ had given me through salvation. I often would find myself reverting back to my old habits, stepping out of His will and purpose for my life to fulfill the lustful desires of this world, backsliding back into bondage. To be honest, the Holy Spirit convicted me through the promptings of my heart; my conscience urged me to resist my sinful desires. I became disconnected from my relationship with God in my backslidden state, grieving the Holy Spirit.

As I continued to grow in my hearing and study of the "Good News" of the Gospel, the Holy Spirit enlightened my understanding of the Word of God, and with my understanding and wisdom of God's Word, the condition of my heart was exposed. The spiritual exposure led me to repent for my backsliding ways, and my repentance led to the reconciliation of my relationship with my Lord and Savior. The Word became a lamp that illuminated the dark path that I was traveling on; the Light enabled me to see my way back to God.

If you find yourself in the state that I have described above, please Stop, Pray, and Ask God to lighten your pathway so He can order your steps with His truth.

**Digging Deeper into the Word** (John 1:1-18)

DAY 1: The Incarnation of God and Word (Logos) (John 1:1-2)
- The Word (Logos) has existed from the beginning of time. (v1a)
- The Word and God coexist together. (v1b)
- God and the Word are the same-person. (v1c)
- The Word (Logos) became spiritual (Jesus, the Holy Spirit) and He was with God from the beginning. (v2)

DAY 2: The Creators (Logos) Spoke (John 1:3-5)
- The Word spoke the universe into existence. (v3a)
- The Spoken Word created everything. (v3b)
- Nothing exists without Him (the Word). (v3c)
- The Word was pregnant with life. (v4a)
- Jesus became the Light of the world—the Savior. (v4b)
- The Word sacrificed himself for the sins of the world. (v5)

DAY 3: Testimony of the Light (John 1:6-13)
- John was sent by God. (v6)
- He was to be a witness to testify of the Light so all would believe. (v7)
- John was not the light, only a witness to it. (v8)
- Jesus, the Light, came to show the world the way to salvation. (v9)
- Due to the world's dark and sinful nature, the world wasn't able to recognize Him. (v10)
- He was rejected by Israel—His chosen people. (v11)
- As believers, we become the children of God. (v12)
- Children are birthed into the Kingdom of God through salvation. (v13)

DAY 4: Jesus: God in the Flesh (John 1:14-18)
- God in the flesh came to dwell with us as Jesus. (v14a)
- God reveals His Glory. (v14b)
- Jesus is the Anointed One, the power of the resurrection. (v14c)
- God's grace and truth is with us in Jesus. (v14d)
- John testified that Jesus is the one. (v15)

- Jesus provides God's grace—forgiveness. (v16)
- Moses' prophesy of salvation is manifested through Jesus Christ. (v17)
- The only way to see God is to accept Christ. (v18a-b)
- Jesus is God in the flesh. (v18c)
- God and Jesus' coexistence is made known through the Word of God. (v18d)

DAY 5: *Tilling the Heart*
Q1: What is your understanding of the Greek word *Logos*?
Q2: How do the Word, God, Holy Spirit, and Jesus coexist? How do you define the Trinity?
Q3: Did God come to the earth in the flesh? How and Why?
Q4: How is Jesus living within you?
Q5: How does your life reflects the Light of Jesus?

## Flowering in the Promises of God
"Then Jesus again spoke to them, saying, 'I am the Light of the world; he who follows Me will not walk in the darkness, but will have the Light of life.'" (John 8:12)

## Morning Glory Prayer
*Heavenly Father, You are alive and powerful. You are the one who sustains my life, and strengthens me with hope and joy. In times of distress I seek You for answers and guidance because You have never failed me. May You richly dwell within me today and forever more. In Jesus' name I pray, Amen.*

## Tending to the Roots
John 1:1-18

## Nourishing with Praise
Fellowship Creative – "Jesus is Alive"
River and Robots – "Lead Me Father (Live at the Mill)"
Phil Wickham – "At Your Name (Yahweh Yahweh)"

Maranatha Music – "Your Great Name"
Bethel – "Lion and the Lamb"

**Bringing in the Harvest**
Psalms 33:6, Psalms 107:20, Psalms 119:89, Psalms 147:15-18,
John 3:19, John 1:14, John 14:9, John 20: 30-31, Acts 17:24-25

# Week 25

## CHRIST IN MY LIFE

### Morning Glory Devotion

"Don't you know that all of us who were baptized into Christ Jesus were baptized into his death? We were therefore buried with him through baptism into death in order that, just as Christ was raised from the dead through the glory of the Father, we too may live a new life." (Romans 6:3-4)

### Growing in God's Word

I had a best friend of twenty-five years who was very special to me. Our friendship bound us together like sisters. We were connected through our children, our hobbies and our love for Christ. Over time our friendship became strained and eventually our connection became broken. There was never any acknowledgment or speaking of the breakup; it was as if our friendship never existed. My attempt to mend our relationship was received with silence. I have prayed many times asking God to reveal to me what happened to our friendship.

The Holy Spirit did reveal to me that I was in a place of offense from rejection, betrayal, and hurt. My heart had become tainted with bitterness and my thoughts of our friendship were consumed by presumption—questioning every motive, analyzing every word spoken, even body gestures, and perceiving them as an attack against me. My thoughts were running wild!

I began to seek God for understanding and forgiveness for what the Holy Spirit had revealed to me. As I meditated on this revelation, I began to understand that forgiveness has many benefits: forgiveness brings peace of mind, spiritually and physically. Forgiveness means releasing the offender(s) of all the sins connected with the offenses. I knew in my heart that I had to forgive my friend of any offense that I believed she had committed against me just as Christ Jesus forgave me of all of my sins that I committed against others and Him.

When I accepted Christ Jesus as my Lord and Savior I had to accept all His attributes. I can't accept forgiveness without forgiving others. True forgiveness is a repentant (sorrowful) heart.

I am a new creation; a child of God, set free and justified by faith no longer under the curse of sin. It's through the love of Christ Jesus that I am truly able to forgive as Christ Jesus forgave and redeemed me to the Father through His death, burial, and resurrection.

My friend and I have apologized to one another for not communicating, but I trust in God that our relationship has been restored through our love for Christ.

**Digging Deeper into the Word** (Romans 6:1-11)

DAY 1: Stop Giving Life to Your Sins; Let Christ Be Alive in You (Romans 6:1-4)
- Grace covers our continued sins, but we should not continue living in them. (v1-2)
- We are united with Christ Jesus in the death of our sins. (v3)
- Our baptism in Christ Jesus is symbolic of our death to sin. (v4a)
- Our baptism in Christ Jesus is symbolic of us being resurrected from the dead with new life, just as Christ was resurrected. (v4b)

DAY 2: There Is Life in Christ (Romans 6:5-6)
- If you are dead to sin you have been justified in Christ. (v5a)
- Born again, you will have eternal life in Christ. (v5b)
- We are no longer under the curse of sin because Christ died for our sins. (v6a)

- We have been redeemed—Set Free—from the bondage of sin. (v6b)

DAY 3: There Is Liberty in Christ (Romans 6:7-8)
- You have been delivered from sin. (v7)
- We now are to live for God's will and for His purpose. (v8)

DAY 4: Life in Christ (Romans 6:9-11)
- He has risen; He is alive. (v9a)
- He made one sacrifice for all time. (v9b)
- Death has no power; it's been defeated. (v9c)
- His crucifixion brought death to sin. (v10a)
- His resurrection brings life to all who believe. (v10b)
- We are dead to sin and alive in Christ. (v11)

DAY 5: *Tilling the Heart*
Q1: Have you been baptized? If not,why? If so, what does your baptism mean?
Q2: How did Christ destroy the curse of sin?
Q3: How are you set free from sins?
Q4: How would you explain what atonement means?
Q5: How do you glorify God in your daily life?

**Flowering in the Promises of God**
"Therefore, if anyone is in Christ, the new creation has come: old has gone, the new is here!" (2 Corinthians 5:17)

**Morning Glory Prayer**
*Heavenly Father, I was buried with You through baptism into death of all my old ways and sins; and, just as You rose from the dead through the glory of the Father, I have a new life. I have been forgiven of my sins, and I freely forgive others as you forgave me. I thank you for the gift of salvation today and for-evermore. In Jesus' name I pray, Amen.*

**Tending to the Roots**
Romans 6:1-11

**Nourishing with Praise**
Vickie Winans – "Because He Lives"
Third Day – "Soul on Fire"
Matt Redman – "Unbroken Praise"
Hillsong United – "Hearts Like Heaven"
William McDowell – "Spirit Break out (ft.) Trinity Anderson"

**Bringing in the Harvest**
Matthew 28:19, Acts 2:24, Galatians 5:24, 1 Peter 4:1, 2
Timothy 2:11, Revelation 1:18, Colossians 3:3

# Week 26

## THE MIND OF CHRIST

**Morning Glory Devotion**
"Do nothing out of selfish ambition or vain conceit. Rather, in humility value others above yourselves, not looking only to your own interests, but each of you to the interests of the others." (Philippians 2:3-4)

**Growing in God's Word**
In 2014, my brother-in-law became very sick requiring 24-hour health care. There wasn't anyone else who was able to take him in to their home and care for him, so my husband and I instantly became homecare providers. Our daily routine and schedule changed completely. We started our day at 5:00 am with my husband bathing and dressing him before leaving for work. Once my husband was finished getting him ready for the day, I would greet him with my daily good morning song, "You are my Sunshine," and I would give my husband his lunch and a goodbye kiss as he walked out the door.

The daily care of my brother-in-law consisted of meal preparations, administering medication, giving him his insulin shots, monitoring his sugar levels throughout the day, assisting him to the bathroom, sometimes cleaning him up and changing his clothes when needed, transporting him to his medical appointments, paying his bills, grocery shopping, etc. Most important, I was there to be a godly companion, ministering the Word of God and praying to keep him encouraged, preserving his dignity.

One day while assisting my brother-in-law in the bathroom he asked me, "How can you bathe and clean a man who is not your husband?" Without pause, I continued to dress him as I looked into his eyes and said, "It's easy; I don't view it as serving man. I'm serving God, which makes it easy to serve because God faithfully serves me. I am humble to know that God trusts me with His child." He responded with a smile and said, "You are a good woman." He died three months later.

We represent God's hands, feet, eyes, ears, and mouth. The Holy Spirit is relying on us to go beyond our comfort zone to answer the call of ministry, servicing one other as Christ served. Say yes to God's calling and let your service be Christ-like with humility, kindness, and with brotherly love. The Holy Spirit will guide and give you the grace needed to fulfill His purpose with excellence and peace of mind.

**Digging Deeper into the Word** (Philippians 2:1-11)

DAY 1: The Call to Be "Christ-Minded (Philippians 2:1-4)
- Through Christ's grace we receive encouragement, comfort, tenderness, and compassion. (v1)
- We are encouraged to demonstrate those Christ-like behaviors. (v2)
- We are warned against selfishness. (v3a)
- We should serve others with humility. (v3b)
- We are called to put other people's needs first. (v4)

DAY 2: Do What Jesus Did: Serve in Humility (Philippians 2:5-6)
- Treat others as Christ would treat them. (v5)
- Jesus is God in the flesh. (v6a)
- Jesus didn't come to be served, but to serve. (6b)

DAY 3: The Ultimate Example of Selfless Humility Displayed (Philippians 2:7-8)
- He lowered himself in status so He could serve. (v7a)
- God appeared in the flesh to man and humbled Himself. (v8a)
- His humility was displayed at the cross. (v8b)

DAY 4: Jesus Exalted by God (Philippians 2:9-11)
- Jesus sits at the right hand of God. (v9a)
- His name is above all names. (v9b)
- The whole creation is subjected to His authority. (v10)
- Every nation will publicly confess that Jesus Christ is Lord. (v11a)
- God the Father will be glorified. (v11b)

DAY 5: *Tilling the Heart*
Q1: How have you been prompted by the Holy Spirit to serve someone who was desperately in need? Did you comply? If yes, what were the circumstances and how did you complete it?
Q2: What does having the mind of Christ mean?
Q3: How do your attitudes toward those in need reflect Christ's message of servanthood?
Q4: What was the last act of service you completed that required humility? How did you respond?
Q5: How has serving others out of humility changed you?

**Flowering in the Promises of God**
"Serve wholeheartedly, as if you were serving the Lord, not people, because you know that the Lord will reward each one for whatever good they do, whether they are slave or free." (Ephesians 6:7-8)

**Morning Glory Prayer**
*Heavenly Father, today I will do nothing out of selfish ambition or vain conceit; but in humility, I will serve the needs of others above my own. In Jesus' name I pray, Amen.*

**Tending to the Roots**
Philippians 2:1-11

**Nourishing with Praise**
Riana Nel – "Lord You Know"
Acappella (Platinum) Aires Junior – "Humble Thyself in the Sight of the Lord"

Passion – "Even So Come (ft.) Kristian Stanfill"
William Murphy – "You are My Strength"
Israel Houghton – "Others"

**Bringing in the Harvest**
2 Corinthians 13:14, Colossians 3:12, Romans 12:16,
Romans 12:10, Galatians 5:26, Matthew 11:29, Romans 8:3,
2 Corinthians 8:9, Hebrews 5:8, Matthew 28:18, Romans
14:11, Romans 14:9

# Week 27

## DON'T LOOK BACK

**Morning Glory Devotion**
"Forget the former things; do not dwell on the past. See, I am doing a new thing! Now it springs up; do you not perceive it? I am making a way in the desert and streams in the wasteland." (Isaiah 43:18-19)

**Growing in God's Word**
Have you ever asked yourself the question, "If I could go back in time, how would I do things differently?" Well, I say, "Why go back?" Your blessings are in front of you, not behind you. What are the benefits of dwelling on the past? There are hidden dangers in looking back on a hopeless past that God has delivered you from. Looking back may cause you to fall into your old sinful ways of thinking and living. Reminiscing on past offenses and un-forgiveness will steal your joy and peace of mind. Sins you have committed in the past can resurface, bringing self-destructive thoughts, condemnation, and guilt you once experienced. For many years I kept asking myself, "How could I stay in an abusive marriage for six years?" I tortured myself with this repeated question. And it wasn't until I came into the full knowledge and understanding of God's word that I was able to release myself from the guilt and shame and finally forgive myself.

God has made a way for us to move forward into our future guilt-free and sin-free. To be forgiven is to forget! Forgiveness is a twofold action; God forgives and forgets, which means NO looking back or re-taking ownership of past failures. If you find yourself always looking back at past mistakes and disappointments, seek God for revelation as to why you continue to focus on the past. Remember, you are a new creation and the old nature is gone. The time is now to release yourself from the past, forgetting the things that are behind and focus on your future in Christ.

**Digging Deeper into the Word** (Isaiah 43:16-21)

DAY 1: Divine Escape (Isaiah 43:16-17)
- God makes a way for escape. (v16a-b)
- God provides instructions for how to defeat the enemy. (v17a)
- Our enemies are defeated through Him. (v17c-d)
- Through God's protection they will never rise up against us again. (v17e-f)

DAY 2: Shift Your Focus (Isaiah 43:18-19)
- Wipe away your past. (v18a)
- Do not reminisce on your past. (v18b)
- Focus on your present and your future. (v19a)
- Look! New beginnings are here. (v19b)
- God restores and sustains our lives. (v19c-d)

DAY 3: Flowing Waters (Isaiah 43:20)
- God sustains nature. (v20a-b)
- God provides plenty of flowing water in barren lands. (v20c-d)
- God provides water for His people on their journey. (v20e-f)

DAY 4: Living in Joy (Isaiah 43:21)
- God delivered His people to serve Him without fear. (v21a)
- Testify to God's goodness for blessing. (v21b)

DAY 5: *Tilling the Heart*
Q1: Describe any past issues that's holding you back from moving forward into your future? If so, explain these issues.

Q2: Why is it so hard for you to let past issues go?

Q3: How can you release those who have wronged you?

Q4: Do you wish you could go back to the way it used to be? Why or why not?

Q5: What are some tangible ways to focus your attention and hopes on what's ahead, rather than what's behind you?

## Flowering in the Promises of God

" 'For I know the plans I have for you,' declares the Lord, 'plans to prosper you and not to harm you, to give you hope and a future.'" (Jeremiah 29:11)

## Morning Glory Prayer

*Heavenly Father, I put my past disappointments behind me and I embrace the new opportunities that You have appointed for me this day that no man can touch. To all of your promises, I say yes and Amen. In Jesus' name I pray, Amen.*

## Tending to the Roots

Isaiah 43:16-21

## Nourishing with Praise

Israel Houghton & New Breed – "Moving Forward"

Ricardo Sanchez (cover) – "It's Not Over"

Travis Green – "Intentional"

Damita – "No Looking Back"

William McDowell – "I Won't Go Back"

## Bringing in the Harvest

Exodus 14:21, Matthew 1 2:20, 2 Corinthians 5 :17, Numbers 20:11, Psalms 148:10, Luke 1:74, 1 Corinthians 10:13

# Week 28

## IN MY FATHER'S CARE

**Morning Glory Devotion**
"The Lord is my shepherd, I shall not be in want. He makes me lie down in green pastures, he leads me beside quiet waters, and he restores my soul. He guides me in paths of righteousness for his name's sake." (Psalms 23:1-3)

**Growing in God's Word**
In 2009, I received notice that my Army job at 1st Armor Training Brigade, Fort Knox, KY had been selected for the government relocation program (the Base Realignment and Closure [BRAC] Program). My organization was scheduled to move to Ft. Benning, Georgia within three years and employees were given a choice to move with the BRAC or take a chance on finding a new job at Fort Knox.

Without hesitation, I announced to my leadership that I was not moving from my home and that I would take my chances at Ft. Knox and began submitting applications for jobs. Three years later I still had no job offers.

I fought this move with every fiber in my body, protesting at town hall meetings, writing grievance letters to the board of appeals. Finally, the time came when I had to make my decision official. I went to God with a heavy heart, angry and crying out to Him, "Why is this happening to me? I have submitted over one hundred job applications during the past three years and I haven't received one job offer." I fervently confessed my dismay to God; "God, I don't want to move from my home and family, and I need a job. I'm tired of fighting this move. Please order my steps and open the door that you want me to walk through and close the door that's not in your perfect will for me. I submit myself fully to the promptings of the Holy Spirit; I will follow." Several days later, after my fervent confession and submission in prayer, I heard clearly– the Holy Spirit tell me, "It's time for your new beginnings, it's time to move." I said, "Yes, Lord, I trust you!"

The moment I said, "I trust you God," an unexplainable peace came over me like I never experienced before. I was moving! Yes, reluctantly to an unfamiliar place that was an eight-hour drive away from my youngest daughter and grandsons, friends, and my church family. I was moving, and the unknown was overwhelming at times, so I would repeat, "I trust you, God!" This confession ceased my fears. Six months later, I arrived at Fort Benning, Georgia. My transition was effortless and stress free; everything fell right into order.

God knew the future blessing He had in store for me. All I had to do was submit and trust in Him. All my blessings from God were connected to the move. Praise God, my home sold within a year, allowing me to make enough profit to get debt free. If I had stayed at Fort Knox, I wouldn't have been able to work enough hours to get debt free. God also used the move to separate me from my worldly distractions and worries that kept me from having a true relationship with Him. With my newfound freedom, I used my time as an opportunity to submit myself to God in complete devotion, with prayer, fasting, and the studying of God's Word. I asked God to purge all the things that were holding me captive, and He did. Praise God! That's when my new beginnings began.

**Digging Deeper into the Word** (Psalms 23:1-6)

DAY 1: In My Father's Care (Psalms 23:1)
- God the "Shepherd" guides and protects. (v1a)
- God the "Sustainer" provides and upholds. (v1b)

DAY 2: He Satisfies Our Every Need (Psalms 23:2-3)
- God keeps me in His peaceful rest. (v2a)
- God keeps peace in my life. (v2b)
- God redeems. (v3a)
- He provides a path to righteousness. (v3b)

DAY 3: Divine Security (Psalms 23:4)
- God is present with my every movement. (v4a)
- God is with me when danger comes. (v4b)
- God is there even to my death. (v4c-d)
- God will guide and defend me. (v4e)
- The Holy Spirit comforts. (v4f)

DAY 4: Divine Provisions (Psalms 23:5-6)
- God provides me with plenty of provisions. (v5a)
- My blessings will not be hindered. (v5b)
- God's favor and divine prosperity are upon me. (v5c)
- The result of God's favor is abundance. (v5d)
- God's favor and comfort will follow me and never flee. (v6a)
- In Him, I have eternal life. (v6b)

DAY 5: *Tilling the Heart*
Q1: How do you deal with unexpected changes in your life?
Q2: Do you seek God's guidance in every situation? Why or why not?
Q3: Have you ever disobeyed a divine assignment from the Holy Spirit because the assignment was too difficult to accept? If yes, explain the results of your decision? If no, what were the blessings of accepting the assignment?
Q4: How do you deal with fear?
Q5: What changes are you willing to make and you haven't submitted to. Why or why not?

**Flowering in the Promises of God**
"For the Lamb at the center of the throne will be their shepherd; he will lead them to springs of living water; and God will wipe every tear from their eyes!" (Revelation 7:17)

**Morning Glory Prayer**

*Heavenly Father, you are my caretaker; the one who provides and protects me. I trust you and where you lead I will follow, through the valley's lows and to the mountain's heights. I will not let fear or pride hinder me from following you. Today, lead me on the path of righteousness for your name's sake. In Jesus' name I pray, Amen.*

**Tending to the Roots**
Psalms 23:1-6

**Nourishing with Praise**
Bethel Music – "Come to Me"
Paul Baloche – "God My Rock"
Chris Tomlin – "Lord I Need You"
Deitrick Haddon – "Trusting God"
Kari Jobe – "The More I Seek You"

**Bringing in the Harvest**
Isaiah 40:11, Ezekiel 34:14, Proverbs 4:11, Isaiah 43:2, Psalms 16:5, Psalms 25:10

## Week 29

### PRIESTHOOD OF BELIEVERS

**Morning Glory Devotion**
"But you are a chosen people, a royal priesthood, a holy nation, God's special possession, that you may declare the praises of him who called you out of darkness into his wonderful light." (1 Peter 2:9)

**Growing in God's Word**
For many years, I served as the Assistant Director for Children's Ministry Vacation Bible School (VBS). I was always very excited about this event from start to finish.  I put my all into getting prepared for it from planning the program to selecting the VBS curriculum. I learned the praise songs and dances we would do each day, set up the game booths, made food selections for the lunch menu, scheduled bus pick-ups and drop-offs, and prepared to host the closing ceremony. Our VBS started on Monday and ran through Friday, from 9:00 a.m. until 1:00 p.m. The kids made the invitations, inviting their parents to the closing ceremony. The VBS summer program was always a success.

When I think back to all the wonderful memories, I fondly recall a conversation I had with a mother of a little girl who attended VBS. This mother explained how excited her daughter was when she came home, sharing all she had learned about Jesus and His love for her. Her daughter explained that even the games had a story about sharing, being honest, and caring for others' feelings. She sang songs about how much God loves her with dancing movements and she mentioned how she was selected to be the teacher's helper. The mother said her daughter's eyes sparkled with every story she shared, and when she came home with an invitation to the VBS closing ceremony, she knew she had to go. She wanted to see for herself what the excitement was all about. During the ceremony, each child was introduced by their teacher as they sang and danced to the VBS songs that they had learned. The children's arts and crafts that they made throughout the week were on display with each child receiving an award for their work. The mother said she understood her little girl's joy and her new love for God. She also wanted to learn more about God with her daughter. She said she would be coming back for church.

We all are called to be minsters of the gospel of Jesus. God used a little girl's excitement to reach her mother's heart. Through the VBS activities, the little girl learned about Jesus' love for her and her responsibility to show that same love toward others. She learned the Word of God through reading and memorizing scriptures, and she learned to sing praise songs about God's love that filled her heart with joy, and that joy lead her mother to church. Not only did her mother come to church, she also accepted Jesus as her Savior and was baptized.

**Digging Deeper into the Word** (1 Peter 2:1-12)

DAY 1: The Fundamentals of Christianity (1 Peter 2:1-5)
- Put off the sins of the flesh. (v1)
- Diligently seek Jesus through the Word of God. (v2)
- New Christians come into the knowledge of the goodness of the Lord through His Word. (v3)
- As you accept Jesus Christ, you will discover the foundation for Christianity. (v4a)
- Jesus was rejected by man. (v4c)
- As Christians, we enter into a priesthood, offering sacrifices to God through Jesus. (v5b)
- As Christians, we live a life of sacrifice acceptable to God. (v5c)

DAY 2: The Precious Stone (1 Peter 2:6-8)
- Old Testament prophesy foretold of the coming of the Savior. (v6a)
- Jesus Christ is the foundation. (v6b)
- Jesus will acknowledge those who trust Him. (v6c)
- The believer is precious in the sight of God. (v7)
- The unbeliever rejects salvation. (v7c)
- The unbeliever is condemned; their unbelief is a stumbling stone and a rock of offense to them. (8a)
- Their offense is being disobedient to the Gospel. (v8b)

DAY 3: A Christian's Purpose (1 Peter 2:9-10)
- We are God's Elect People. (v9a-c)
- We are to give God all the praise for His goodness throughout the world. (v9d)
- We were once in darkness and now are in the light. (v10a)
- We weren't under grace, and now we receive His mercy. (v10b)

DAY 4: Be Living Witness for Christ (1 Peter 2:11-12)
- Depart from sins. (v11a)
- Let your Holy lifestyle be a testimony to the unbelievers. (v12a)
- Live by Christian principles, giving unbelievers no room to speak reproach against you. (v12b)
- Let your Christian actions lead others to Jesus. (v12c)

DAY 5: *Tilling the Heart*

Q1: In what ways do you diligently seek God?

Q2: How do you define Royal Priesthood?

Q3: How have your Christian actions or lack of Christian actions caused an unbeliever to question your commitment to your faith?

Q4: Have you ever lead anyone to Christ? If so, what were the circumstances? If not, why?

Q5: How do you serve as a minister to others?

**Flowering in the Promises of God**
"So this is what the Sovereign Lord says: 'See, I lay a stone in Zion, a tested stone, a precious cornerstone for a sure foundation; the one who relies on it will never be stricken with panic.'" (Isaiah 28:16)

**Morning Glory Prayer**
*Heavenly Father, I thank you for choosing me as your elect and for making me precious in your sight. Strengthen me in my walk with you so my lifestyle will be a living testimony for you. Today, I commit myself to you fully. In Jesus' name I pray, Amen.*

**Tending to the Roots**
1 Peter 2:1-12

**Nourishing with Praise**
Chris Tomlin – "Chosen Generation"
God's Chosen – "Love Medley"
Israel Houghton – "In Jesus Name"
Todd Dulaney – "Victory Belongs to Jesus"

**Bringing in the Harvest**
Psalms 118:22-24, Isaiah 8:14-15, Isaiah 53:1-9 Romans 15:16, 1 Corinthians 3:9, Ephesians 2:1-22, Psalms 118:22, Isaiah 8:14, Deuteronomy 7:6, Hosea 2:23, Galatians 5:16, Philippians 2:15

# Week 30

## FATHER, NOT MY WILL, BUT YOURS

### Morning Glory Devotion

"Watch and pray so that you will not fall into temptation. The spirit is willing, but the flesh is weak." (Matthew 26:41)

### Growing in God's Word

While preparing this devotional I experienced bittersweet emotions knowing that Jesus Christ went through such agony and grief on my behalf because He loves me. It was in my ignorance that I thought that Jesus didn't understand my pain, my suffering, and the continuous attacks from the devil that were trying to destroy my life. I knew Jesus suffered; but, it wasn't until I studied these scriptures on the account of His last prayer in the Garden of Gethsemane before being betrayed by one of His own, that I realized my thinking on the degree to which He suffered was in error.

The truth is, Jesus bore "every pain" that's upon the face of the earth, every disease known and unknown to man, every mental illness, every mental and physical anguish; He bore every affliction. We, as Christians, are enjoying the benefits of Jesus Christ taking all of our sins to the cross. As a result of His agonizing death, the redeemed have access to all the promises of God—the abundance of joy, perfect peace, and prosperity. I'm so grateful that in His human weakness He was determined to fulfill His purpose and He humbled Himself so God's perfect will would be done on the cross.

**Digging Deeper into the Word** (Matthew 26: 36-46)

DAY 1: In the Garden of Agony (Matthew 26:36-37)
- Jesus set an example for us as He went to the Garden to pray and commune with God. (v36)
- Jesus loves us and grieves when we do not honor Him. (v37)

DAY 2: Jesus Prayed to the Father (Matthew 26:38-39)
- In His hour of distress, Jesus and His inner circle prayed. (v38)
- Jesus humbled Himself and prayed alone. (v39a)
- In reverence to God, Jesus' prayer signifies how much His soul was in anguish. (v39b)
- Jesus prayed that God's will be done. (v39c)

DAY 3: His Agony Confirms His Sufferings (Matthew 26:40-42)
- Jesus felt betrayed when He found His inner circle sleeping and not praying. (v40a)
- Jesus questioned Peter's commitment to prayer. (v40b)
- Jesus declared that prayer preserves men from temptation. (v41a)
- In the flesh, we are weak even though our spirit may be willing to do as God commands. (v41b)
- Jesus persisted in prayer. (v42a)
- He prayed for deliverance for His anguish. (v42b)
- Jesus prayed for God's will to prevail. (v42c)

DAY 4: It's Time (Matthew 26:43-46)
- Jesus found His inner circle for the second time unwilling to press through in prayer. (v43)
- Jesus prayed with determination the same prayer: God let your will be done. (v44)
- Jesus questioned His inner circle again about their commitment to prayer. (v45a)
- Jesus foretells His betrayal. (v45b)
- Jesus sees the one who would betray Him. (v46)

DAY 5: *Tilling the Heart*
Q1: What is the will of God for your life?
Q2: What role does prayer play in your life? What changes do you need to make to pray more?
Q3: Why did Jesus insist on His disciples watching and praying with Him?
Q4: What was the explanation that Jesus gave for why men should always pray?
Q5: Why was Jesus feeling overwhelmed with anguish in the garden of Gethsemane? What did He pray about? Who did He pray to?

## Flowering in the Promises of God
"But God demonstrates his own love for us in this: While we were still sinners, Christ died for us." (Romans 5:8)

## Morning Glory Prayer
*Heavenly Father, keep me observant and strong so I'm able to pray wholeheartedly and reveal any distractions that may hinder my prayer life. Today, filter my prayers and breathe life on my words so they will line up with your Word and for your prefect will to be done in me. In Jesus' name I pray, Amen.*

## Tending to the Roots
Matthew 26:36-46

## Nourishing with Praise
Danielle Rose – "The Agony in the Garden"
Fred Hammond – "Clean Heart"
Anne Murray – "In the Garden"
Donald Lawrence ft. Faith Evans – "Say a Prayer"
Sidewalk Prophets – "You Will Never Leave Me"

## Bringing in the Harvest
Mark 14:32, Mark 5:37, John 12:27, John 6:38, Matthew 20:22, John 13:1

## Week 31

### THE SUSTAINER

**Morning Glory Devotion**
"Come to me, all you who are weary and burdened, and I will give you rest." (Matthew 11:28)

**Growing in God's Word**
As a single mother with three children and an income that left no room for financial error, it was difficult to be a good steward over money that I didn't really have. I didn't make enough money to sustain my family from the start, but financial hardship taught me to trust in God.

I had a system that ensured all of my monthly bills would be paid by their due dates. Often, unexpected expenses would come up causing me to shuffle bill payments around to avoid going into default on some and to prevent other essential services from being disconnected. I can remember one particular time when I got paid on a Friday and the monthly bills were due. Once I paid the essential bills, I found myself with no money to buy groceries. I calculated my expenses on paper trying to figure out where and why I came up short, or in this case, without money to buy groceries. Regardless of the reasons for the shortfall, I was still in need of grocery money.

So, I did something different this time, I took my need to God in prayer, believing He would come through for me. As I prayed, I said, *Lord, you sit high and look low; you know all of my needs even before I do. I have no money, no food, and three children to feed. I have used up all my dependable sources who have helped me in the past to the point that they are now avoiding me, not taking my calls or answering my text or email messages. Father, you are my only source, and I trust you to care and provide for us, Amen.* I got up from making my petition known to God with full confidence that He would help.

After praying that prayer the very Sunday of payday week, the children and I went to church as usual, and when we returned home, the Holy Spirit prompted me to go to the mailbox. I thought, *It's Sunday, and I'm sure I checked the mailbox on Saturday. Besides, if there is mail, it's only bills and that can wait!* A couple of hours passed and the Holy Spirit prompted me again. I finally gave in, and when I opened the mailbox door, there was a white envelope with no address or name on it. I opened the envelope immediately and, to my surprise, there was one thousand dollars inside the envelope. Not only did I have enough money to buy groceries, but I was able to get other necessities that we had become accustomed to not having as well. Many years later, the Holy Spirit revealed to me the person who blessed my family on that day, and we are still very dear friends.

When you trust in God, not knowing when or how He will provide for your needs, watch how God makes a way. God moves on the hearts of people to answer the prayers of others. His provisions come in many different forms, such as peace of mind, joy, and godly confidence that He will take care of His own.

**Digging Deeper into the Word** (Matthew 11:25-30)

DAY 1: God's Goodness (Matthew 11:25-26)
- Jesus gives God Praise: For justice and mercy and for revelation of God made known to the wise and unlearned. (v25)
- Jesus gave thanks to the Father for His good will. (v26)

DAY 2: God Only (Matthew 11:27-28)
- Jesus Christ has all power in His hands. (v27a-b)
- The full understanding of the Godhead is made known

through the gospel illumination of scriptures and revelation knowledge. (v27c)
- Jesus invites all to come: the weary, the burdened, the poor, the sick, the diseased, the broken-hearted, the sinner, the lame, the blind, the deaf, etc. (v28a)
- In Him, they find rest that only God can give. (v28b)

DAY 3: The Giver of Rest (Matthew 11:29)
- Give your concerns and your load to God. (v29a)
- The effects of righteousness are peace and humility. (v29b)
- We have divine serenity through Him. (v29c)

DAY 4: The Way of the Lord Is Easy (Matthew 11:30)
- God's method is profitable and fulfilling to your mind, heart, soul, and spirit. (v30)

DAY 5: *Tilling the Heart*
Q1: How has God provided for you in hard times?
Q2: What financial blessing have you received?
Q3: What do you do in times of financial hardship?
Q4: Are you experiencing any financial burdens? If yes, how are you dealing with it? If not, how do you manage your finances to prevent unexpected hardship?
Q5: Do you seek God in your monthly budgeting? If yes, how? If no, why?

**Flowering in the Promises of God**
"And my God will meet all your needs according to the riches of his glory in Christ Jesus." (Philippians 4:19)

**Morning Glory Prayer**
*Heavenly Father, teach me how to be a good steward over my money and be trustworthy with it. I want to be a lender, not a borrower, and position me to receive the overflow so I can be a blessing to those in need. Today, in Jesus' name I declare the favor of God in my life. In Jesus' name I pray, Amen.*

**Tending to the Roots**
Matthew 11:25-30

**Nourishing with Praise**
Mandisa – "Overcomer"
Earnest Pugh – "Rain on Us"
Tamela Mann – "Take Me to the King"
William Murphy – "Praise Is What I Do"

**Bringing in the Harvest**
Job 37:24, John 12:27, Matthew 28:18, Isaiah 28:12, Jeremiah 31:25, 1 John 5:3

# Week 32

## THE BLESSINGS FOR OBEDIENCE

**Morning Glory Devotion**
"In all thy ways acknowledge him, and he shall direct thy paths." (Proverbs 3:6 KJV)

**Growing in God's Word**
When my best friend of eight years asked for my hand in marriage, I said yes! We were married soon after. I lived in Georgia and my husband lived in Alabama. We both were civilian employees working for the US Army. Immediately, we began our search for a job that would allow me to transfer to Alabama.

Meanwhile, we alternated every other weekend driving back and forth between Georgia and Alabama. Several months passed by without any job offers. One day at work while sitting at my desk, I asked God, *Why haven't I been offered a job in Alabama?* I began to remind God that it was not in His Will for a husband and wife to live apart, then I said, *It couldn't be my resume or my job application. My duty responsibilities are written perfectly and my office management skills have increased immensely. God, I don't understand why I'm still in Georgia waiting?*

I heard the Holy Spirit saying, *Change your prayer.* I whispered to myself what I heard, "Change my prayer?" I meditated on these words for a while, and I thought, *What is my prayer concerning moving to be with my husband?* Immediately, my "want list" came to mind and I begin to list them all to God.

The Holy Spirit had to intercede so I could shift my thinking about what my prayer should be. I prayed, *Lord, where you lead me I will go. Place me where you want me to be, where I can be my very best and glorify you. In Jesus name, I pray. Amen.* I was prompted by the Holy Spirit to do an eight-hour fast the following work day. I called my husband and shared with him the revelation that I received from the Holy Spirit. He offered to join me in the fast. I thanked him for the offer, but told him, "No, this fast is just for me, but please keep me up in prayer. After the fast, I will let you know what I receive from God."

At the end of my workday and the end of my fast, and I was preparing to go home when I heard the Holy Spirit say, "Retirement." I chuckled and repeated what I heard, "Retirement?" I prayed, *God if this is my emotion reacting, please shut it down but, if this is from you, please confirm your Word.*

My husband called me before I could leave the office and asked, "Well, did you hear from God?" I replied, "Yes, I literally got a word, and it was *retirement.*" My husband responded with excitement, "Retirement? Praise God! How do you feel about it?" I replied, "I'm excited, but . . . ," before I could complete my answer, he interrupted me and said with great confidence, "If you are concerned about money, don't be; we can afford it! So, whenever God opens that retirement door, we will be fine." His words brought a big smile to my face.

Three days later, I received an email from the Department of the Army. The email subject line read "It's Finally Here!" I opened the email and began to read it and discovered that the Army was offering the Volunteer Early Retirement Program (VERP) for a limited time to people within my Fort Benning, Georgia organization, the US Army Maneuver Center of Excellence. There were four criteria outlined in order to qualify for the program.

My heart was pounding with excitement, I called my husband before reading the four requirements and, as I read them aloud to him, I found I met all the requirements! Praise

God, three months later, I retired with full benefits. My last day of work in Georgia was my first day living with my husband under the same roof. I prayed for God's guidance; I obeyed the promptings of the Holy Spirit to fast; I submitted my will to God's Will; I believed wholeheartedly that God would work on our behalf concerning our marriage; I waited in faith. My obedience was greatly rewarded far beyond anything that I could ever imagine. Hallelujah! Praise Jesus!

Retirement has allowed me time to carry out the work of the ministry as the founder of Ladies Adorned by Christ & Empowered (L.A.C.E.), a women's Bible study and intercessory prayer group that I host weekly. Additionally, I have the time to write this devotional book, which I have put off for the last fifteen years. I now devote my time to God, giving Him my best service.

**Digging Deeper into the Word (Proverbs 3:1-10)**

DAY 1: The Wisdom of a Father: Living by the Word (Proverbs 3:1-3)
- Obey and meditate on God's instructions. (v1)
- Obedience will be rewarded with long life and peace. (v2)
- Always preserve love, faithfulness, mercy, and truth. (v3a)
- Clothe your mind with the commandments of God. (v3b)
- Out of the Heart, comes the issues of life, so engrave His commandments on your heart. (3bc)

DAY 2: The Word Produces Godly Character (Proverb 3:4-6)
- Godly character obtains acceptance with people and favor with God will be increased. (v4)
- Trust wholeheartedly that God knows what's best. (v5a)
- Turn away from your wisdom and trust God's wisdom. (v5b)
- Submit to the Father and He will order your steps. (v6)

DAY 3: Wisdom Promotes Good Health (Proverbs 3:7-8)
- Avoid pridefulness and high-mindedness. (v7a)
- Revere God and He will keep you from the evil one. (v7b)
- Wisdom strengthens your body and prolongs your life. (v8)

DAY 4: With Obedience: Comes Overflow (Proverb 3:9-10)
- Honor God with the first fruits of your increase. (v9)
- The abundance of God's blessings are promised. (v10)

DAY 5: *Tilling the Heart*
Q1: How do you know you are hearing from the Holy Spirit?
Q2: What does praying amiss mean?
Q3: How do you accept spiritual correction?
Q4: What is the biblical meaning of first fruits?
Q5: What are the benefits of obedience?

**Flowering in the Promises of God**
"The LORD will send a blessing on your barns and on everything you put your hand to. The LORD your God will bless you in a land he is giving you. The LORD will establish you as his holy people, as he promised you on oath, if you keep the commands of the LORD your God and walk in his ways." (Deuteronomy 28:8-9)

**Morning Glory Prayer**
*Heavenly Father, without you, I'm nothing; but, with you, I'm an overcomer. You have blessed my coming in and going out. I will keep your commands and walk in your ways. Today, I thank you for overflowing blessings that have come to me through obedience. In Jesus' name, I pray. Amen.*

**Tending to the Roots**
Proverbs 3:1-10

**Nourishing with Praise**
Lauren Daigle – "Trust in You"
Hezekiah Walker – "Breakthrough"
William McDowell – "Withholding Nothing"
Shekinah – "Say Yes"
Marvin Sapp – "He Has His Hands on You"

**Bringing in the Harvest**
Deuteronomy 30:16, Psalms 91:16, Psalms 111:10, Proverbs 9:10, Exodus 20:6, 2 Samuel 15:20, Luke 2:52, Jeremiah 9:23, Philippians 4:6, Romans 12:16

## Week 33

CHRISTIAN CONDUCT

**Morning Glory Devotion**

"Make it your ambition to lead a quiet life, to mind your own business and to work with your hands, just as we told you, so that your daily life may win the respect of outsiders and so that you will not be dependent on anybody." (1 Thessalonians 4:11-12)

**Growing in God's Word**

Does your Christian walk match your confession of faith in Christ Jesus? Are you being a witness in your daily living for Christ or are you walking around with a big "S" on your chest declaring, "I'm Saved," while your actions show no evidence of the "Power of Christ" in your life?

I'll never forget the encounter my oldest daughter had at school when she was thirteen years old. She came home from school very emotional, and, while fighting back tears, she told me, "Mom, I was standing in the lunch line and a boy was standing in front of me at the cash register when the lunch lady checked our lunch account to ensure we had enough money to pay for our lunches. The boy in front of me has a reduced lunch account like me. His account balance was zero and he only needed forty cents to pay for his lunch. The lady yelled out, 'Didn't I tell you not to come back until you get money on your account?' He explained that his mom wouldn't get paid until next week and she would put money on the account then. So, he said to her, 'Could you please let me eat because I'm hungry?' The lady, yelled at him, 'You're already getting lunch at a reduced price! Can't you afford forty cents? Get out of my line

and don't come back until you have money on your account!'"
Every student in proximity heard the belittling remarks she said
to him, and it made my daughter sad.

"Mom, I spoke up and said, 'I have enough money I will
pay for his lunch!' The lady said, 'You didn't have to do that,' and
I said, 'Yes, I do.' I paid for our lunches. With tears in his eyes, he
thanked me and walked away. Mom, I was very respectful to the
lady but, I said to her, 'You told me that you were a Christian,
but that's not how a Christian acts. You should be ashamed of
yourself,' and I walked away in tears."

I comforted my daughter and praised her for doing
what was right. I explained to her that we shouldn't say we
are Christian and then do hurtful things to others. But, praise
God, Ebony displayed the values of love and empathy of a
true Christian to that boy, and I hope that the lunch lady was
convicted to repentance for her unchristian–like conduct.

Don't let your ungodly actions hinder your Christian
walk. Be a living witness for Christ, showing others the same
mercy and grace that was shown to you by our Lord and Savior.

**Digging Deeper into the Word** (1 Thessalonians 4:1-12)

DAY 1: God's Vessels of Honor (1 Thessalonians 4:1-4)
- We are given instructions on holy living. (v1)
- If you are not ignorant of the preached Word of God, a higher standard of living is required of you. (v2)
- God's will for us is that His Children be set apart. (v3)
- We are to present our bodies as instruments of righteousness and honor for God's usage. (v4)

DAY 2: Live Honorably (1 Thessalonians 4:5-7)
- Believers have been liberated by Jesus from the works of the flesh. (v5)
- There will be consequences for those who take advantage of other Christians. (v6)
- God calls us to holiness. (v7)

DAY 3: Love: Your Life's Guiding Principle (1 Thessalonians 4:8-10)
- Rejecting God's Word means your rejection of the Holy Spirit. (v8)
- God has demonstrated His love for us through Christ's death for the sins of the world. (v9)
- Extend your love to all with patience and diligence as Christ does with you. (v10)

Day 4: Live a Blameless Life (1 Thessalonians 4:11-12)
- Live in peace intentionally. (v11a)
- Don't be a busybody, be useful in your works. (v11b)
- Let your Christian lifestyle be your witness for Christ. (v12a)
- Solely depend on God. (v12b)

DAY 5: *Tilling the Heart*
Q1: How has your actions ever hindered you from being an effective witness for Christ? What did you do? How did you overcome it?
Q2: What is your most effective way of leading?
Q3: When have you come to the aid of a person in need?
Q4: How did you show empathy toward others?
Q5: When you are in the wrong how do you make it right?

**Flowering in the Promises of God**
"You are the light of the world. A town built on a hill cannot be hidden. Neither do people light a lamp and put it under a bowl. Instead they put it on its stand, and it gives light to everyone in the house. In the same way, let your light shine before others, that they may see your good deeds and glorify your Father in heaven." (Matthew 5:14-16)

**Morning Glory Prayer**
*Heavenly Father, by your Holy Spirit, continue to order my steps, my words, and my conduct so I can live an honorable life. I will work with my hands in a useful and honorable way as*

113

*commanded. Let my character and lifestyle win the respect of others for your name's sake. Today, I will be mindful of others feelings, showing them the same mercy and grace You have shown me. In Jesus' name, I pray. Amen.*

**Tending to the Roots**
1 Thessalonians 4:1-12

**Nourishing with Praise**
Brandon Heath – "I'm Not Who I Was"
Hillsong United – "All for Love"
Fred Hammond – "Keeping My Mind"
Chris Tomlin – "Jesus (Simplified)"
Marvin Winans & The Praise Choir – "Walk Like Jesus"

**Bringing in the Harvest**
2 Corinthians 13:11, 1 Corinthians 6:18, Romans 1:24, Galatians 4:8, Romans 12:19, 1 Peter 1:15, 1 John 3:24, John 13:34,  2 Thessalonians 3:10, Colossians 4:5

# Week 34

## GETTING WISDOM

**Morning Glory Devotion**

"When tempted, no one should say, 'God is tempting me.' For God cannot be tempted by evil, nor does he tempt anyone; but each person is tempted when they are dragged away by their own evil desire and enticed." (James 1:13-14)

**Growing in God's Word**

I was sitting on my couch contemplating, "How will I respond when people ask me about the whereabouts of my youngest daughter?" My heart was overwhelmed with sorrow and shame. My baby girl was in prison and pregnant with her second child. I spoke my thoughts out loud to God and said, "How can I bear this pain of hopelessness day-by-day until her release and also be able to answer questions when asked about her current situation without bitterness or out of anger, revealing my shame?"

The presence of the Holy Spirit ushered in and brought comfort to my spirit with tender words of love that touched my heart. The answer was revealed in my spirit; "Tell them that your daughter is in the very best of care, she is hanging out with Mercy and Grace!" Instantly, God's blessed assurance conquered my hopelessness and the shame I felt was removed from my heart with His Words of "Mercy and Grace." I knew right at that moment that my unborn grandbaby would be healthy and that my beautiful daughter was going to receive her deliverance and her faith would be restored.

The following Sunday, after church services, I was walking out the door when a few of my closest church friends called out my name, very eager to talk to me. As they approached, I heard in my spirit the words "Mercy and Grace." "Hello, how are you, they asked?" I responded, "I'm well!" Another question followed, "So, how is your daughter, Jasmine?" I smiled and said, "She is great! She is hanging out with 'Mercy and Grace,' she's in good company!" They all looked at me with great surprise, and they replied, "Great," as I walked away. I said to myself, "Thank you, God, for discernment and your words of wisdom."

Three weeks later, a sister from church wanted to share a praise report with me. She said, "Do you remember three weeks ago when a group of women approached you asking about your daughter, even though they already knew the situation?" "Yes," I said, "I do remember." She smiled and explained, "Well, I was standing a little distance off, but close enough to hear the conversation. Your response that your daughter was hanging out with 'Mercy and Grace' shut down the chatter. I want to thank you because a week later, after overhearing that conversation, now, my daughter is hanging out with 'Mercy and Grace' and the words you spoke gave me peace."

The Holy Spirit comforted me with His words of wisdom that brought healing and peace to my heart. The peace of God gave me confidence in knowing that the Lord had her situation under control. Not only was He with me during this troublesome time for our family, but also with my daughter and her unborn son. Today, my daughter is restored and living for Jesus and my grandson is eight years old, strong and healthy.

**Digging Deeper into the Word** (James 1:2-18)

DAY 1: Trials and Tribulations: Toughen Your Faith (James 1:2-8)
- Count everything you encounter as joy. (v2)
- The testing of your faith builds patience. (v3)
- Let patience work in you. (v4)
- Pray for the wisdom of God. (v5)
- Pray without doubting. (v6)
- Be steadfast in your prayers. (v7)
- Uncertainty leads to wavering faith. (v8)

DAY 2: Worldly Riches vs. Spiritual Blessings (James 1:9-12)
- God blesses the humble. (v9)
- Worldly riches are temporary. (v10)
- Earthly possessions and wealth will dry up. (v11)
- Believers who endure will receive the crown of life. (v12)

DAY 3: God Doesn't Tempt You, He Tests You (James 1:13-16)
- God doesn't entice man with evil. (v13)
- You are tempted with the lust that's already in your heart. (v14)
- Don't be deceived, for the wages of sin is death. (v15-16)

DAY 4: God's Giving Is Perfect (James 1:17-18)
- Every good and perfect gift comes from above. (v17a)
- God is infallible and unchangeable; God gives us what is good and not evil. (v17b)
- God purposely and intentionally gave us life through His spoken Word. (v18a)
- All authority and wealth upon the earth is given to the Children of God. (v18b)

DAY 5: *Tilling the Heart*
Q1: How do you seek wisdom and from whom?
Q2: What situation have you experience in your life that you were too ashamed to be able to talk about?
Q3: What is the meaning of infallible?
Q4: When have you ever blamed God for falling into temptation? Looking back, do you still believe that it was God who tempted you? Why or why not?
Q5: Why is having godly wisdom important?

**Flowering in the Promises of God**
"For I will give you words and wisdom that none of your adversaries will be able to resist or contradict." (Luke 21:15)

**Morning Glory Prayer**

*Heavenly Father, deliver me from my own evil desires that drag me into temptation. Give me discernment when enticing spirits try to overtake me. Give me a soft word to answer those who are stirring up trouble. Today, I will resist gossiping and lewd spirits. In Jesus' name, I pray. Amen.*

**Tending to the Roots**
James 1:2-18

**Nourishing with Praise**
Christ Tomlin – "I Will Rise – The Wisdom of God"
Laura Woodley Osman – "Wisdom Song"
Crabb Family – "Through the Fire"
Worship Video – "I See Grace"
Amanda Cook/Brave New World – "Mercy"

**Bringing in the Harvest**
James 3:17, Matthew 21:21, James 4:8, Luke 14:11, 1 Corinthians 7:31, Isaiah 40:7, Luke 6:22, Job 15:35

## Week 35

### HEALING A NATION

**Morning Glory Devotion**

"If my people, who are called by my name, will humble themselves and pray and seek my face and turn from their wicked ways, then I will hear from heaven, and I will forgive their sin and will heal their land." (2 Chronicles 7:14)

**Growing in God's Word**

The 2016 Senate and Presidential Election was the worst negative campaigning I have witnessed in my lifetime. The campaign speeches laced with hatred and advertisements filled with lies literally drove a wedge through the heart of our nation. This intentional mistrust to pit the nation's people against each other led to a deeply divided nation on issues such as social/economic fairness, tax breaks for the rich, racism, freedom of religion, cultural inferiority, gender and sexual orientation inequality, business tax breaks, voter registration suppression, immigration policy, building of a wall, an unequal justice system that tilts against the poor and minorities, and the list of divisions continues on to the point that it has even set families and friends against each other. My husband and I felt so sick in our spirit from all the bullying campaign tactics that we stopped watching the news. But, what was more disturbing and appalling than the campaign tactics was to see how God's chosen people—"Christians"—freely spewed racial hatred toward their neighbors who didn't believe or look like them. We sought God through prayer and fasting, asking Him to expose the condition of His people's hearts and to heal our nation.

Several weeks later, on November 10, 2016, we felt the promptings of the Holy Spirit, leading us during our devotional study time to read Chapter 7 of 2 Chronicles. When reading verse 14, we felt strongly to start praying for healing and unity for our country, and for a smooth transition of presidential power from President Barack Obama to the newly elected President Donald Trump. We also prayed for our military, police departments, and first responders. As we finished our devotional study and prayer, we had no doubt that this was the start of a God-given assignment to pray continuously for our nation, so we began a seventy-two-day Prayer Challenge that started on Veteran's Day, November 11, 2016 and ended on Inauguration Day, January 20, 2017. Each morning my husband and I got up around 5:00 a.m. to pray live on Facebook and YouTube. During the prayer challenge, God revealed to us that our Christian nation lacked brotherly love, and that Christians were neglecting their Christian duty by putting their political ideology ahead of their Christian obligation for humility and service to each other. We believe that if our nation is to receive its complete healing, the hearts of God's people have to change and we must begin truly loving each other and focus daily on fulfilling God's purpose on the earth.

**Digging Deeper into the Word** (2 Chronicles 7:11-22)

DAY 1: The Glory of the Lord Filled the Temple (2 Chronicles 7:11-13)
- Because of Solomon's faithfulness, the Lord chose the temple Solomon built as His own. (v11-12)
- God chooses faithful servants to deliver a warning to His people. (v13)

DAY 2: God's Conditions for Healing a Nation (2 Chronicles 7:14-16)
- As in Israel, we must humble ourselves, pray, seek God's righteousness, repent, and turn from our wickedness.

(v14a)
- Our reward for meeting God's Conditions is that He will hear our prayers and His forgiveness will be extended to us and He will heal our nation. (V14b)
- God will be attentive to the prayers of His people. (v15)
- The Almighty God will abide in His temple forever. (v16)

DAY 3: Faithfulness Rewarded (2 Chronicles 7:17-18)
- Stay faithful to God by obeying all He has commanded, according to His Word. (v17)
- God will keep His covenant with His people. (v18)

DAY 4: Consequences of Disobedience (2 Chronicles 7:19-22)
- God warns us of the consequences for disobedience. (v19)
- God foretells of our punishment. (v20)
- God punishes the disobedience of His people. (v21)
- Our disobedience will bring disaster upon us. (v22)

DAY 5: *Tilling the Heart*
Q1: Who are God's chosen people?
Q2: How important is prayer to you?
Q3: How do you deal with worldly conflicts?
Q4: How often do you pray for our nation and its leaders? What specifically do you pray for?
Q5: Do you believe in the power of prayer? Explain why or why not?

**Flowering in the Promises of God**
"But you are a chosen group of people. You are the King's religious leaders. You are a holy nation. You belong to God. He has done this for you so you can tell others how God has called you out of darkness into His great light. At one time you were a people of no use. Now you are the people of God. At one time you did not have loving-kindness. Now you have God's loving-kindness." (1 Peter 2:9-10)

**Morning Glory Prayer**

*Heavenly Father, your word says that if your people who are called by your name would humble themselves and pray and seek your face and turn from their wicked ways, then you will hear from Heaven, and you will forgive their sins and will heal their land. Father, we humble ourselves before you and we surrender our will to seek your righteousness. Father, we come to you on behalf of our nation. We ask you to forgive our nation's sins of hatred, idolatry, murder of the innocent, division, abandoning of the poor and sick, and turning from your commandments. Lord, we need you to heal our nation of all its wickedness. I pray your people will come to know your revelation knowledge of who you are. Today, forgive us of our sins and heal our nation, restore the brightness of your love and grace as our guiding principle, letting unity, peace, and brotherly love, once again, be the fruit of our nation. In Jesus' name, I pray, Amen.*

**Tending to the Roots**
2 Chronicles 7:1-22

**Nourishing with Praise**
Planetshakers – "Heal Our Land (Live)"
Mark Conner – "Heal Our Nation (Medley)"
Gary Sadler – "Heart for The Nation (Medley)"
Planetshahakers – "The Anthem (Full Song)"
Casting Crowns – "If We Are the Body (Acoustic)"

**Bringing in the Harvest**
Psalms 33:12, James 4:6, Psalms 33:16-19, Psalms 115:1, 1 Timothy 2:1-4, 1 Corinthians 3:16-17, 1 Corinthians 6: 19-20, 2 Corinthians 6:16, Ephesians 2:19-22, 1 Peter 2:5

# Week 36

## NEWNESS OF LIFE

**Morning Glory Devotion**
"So, then, just as you received Christ Jesus as Lord, continue to live your lives in him, rooted and built up in him, strengthened in the faith as you were taught, and overflowing with thankfulness." (Colossians 2:6-7)

**Growing in God's Word**
When I held my firstborn grandbaby in my arms for the very first time, my perception of new life took on a whole new meaning. I smiled as I inspected his little body, and with great wonder, I confirmed, "Yes, Lord, how great is your creation of mankind. We truly are fearfully and wonderfully made!"

We are born with no instincts other than to grow, trusting with pure hearts and minds; we totally depend on our parents for all of our needs. A baby's identity is defined by their innocence with no history of misconduct or acts of self-hatred caused by deceit from negative words, abuse, and worldly traditions. The newborn baby's life and self-image has not been defiled by man's wicked ways.

Our accepting Christ Jesus as our Lord and Savior redeems us from our past of sin and acts of evil; they are forgotten and we are forgiven. Our salvation is like the birth of a newborn baby—there is no history of misconduct to report.

Our rebirth through Christ Jesus is newness of life, undefiled by man. We learn our true identity. We grow in the knowledge of God's Word. We reject man's beliefs and worldly traditions. We depend on the instructions of God to lead us, to protect us, and to have life more abundantly while on Earth and eternal life in Christ. May you overflow with thankfulness to Christ Jesus for your new birth in Him!

**Digging Deeper into the Word** (Colossians 2:6-14)

DAY 1: Christian Growth (Colossians 2:6-8)
- Having received Christ as your Savior, stand firm in His instructions. (v6)
- Grow and increase in the knowledge of God through the Holy Spirit. (v7a-b)
- Allow your thankfulness to overflow. (v7c)
- Be alert, don't be deceived by man's beliefs or worldly traditions. (v8a)
- Don't put your faith in human nature, rejecting God's nature. (v8b)

DAY 2: The Nature of God (Colossians 2:9-10)
- The fullness of the "Godhead" came to us through Christ. (v9)
- We are partakers in the fullness of Christ. (v10)

DAY 3: Divine Conversion (Colossians 2:11-12)
- Christ is the mediator between God and man. (v11a)
- Reject fleshly sin and accept Christ's Salvation. (v11b)
- Baptism represents our acceptance of the death, burial, and resurrection of our Lord and Savior. (v12)

DAY 4: Blotted Out the Written Law (Colossians 2: 13-14)
- We once were dead but now are reconciled back to Christ. (v13)
- Jesus was the fulfillment of the Law at the cross. (v14)

DAY 5: *Tilling the Heart*
Q1: How do you grow in the knowledge of God?
Q2: How would you describe the meaning of Godhead?
Q3: How do you obtain the newness of life through Christ Jesus?
Q4: What is it meant by blotting out God's written ordinances?

Q5: What are you thankful for in Christ Jesus? Why?

**Flowering in the Promises of God**
"Whatever you have learned or received or heard from me, or seen in me—put it into practice. And the God of peace will be with you." (Philippians 4:9)

**Morning Glory Prayer**
*Heavenly Father, keep me rooted in your Word as I live my life, strengthening my faith as I continue to understand and learn your ways. My heart is filled with unspeakable joy; today I'm overflowing with thankfulness toward you. In Jesus' name I pray, Amen.*

**Tending to the Roots**
Colossians 2:6-14

**Nourishing with Praise**
Christian K. – "God of New Beginnings"
Audrey Assad – "New Every Morning"
Linda Clark – "New Beginnings"
Kurt Carr – "Just the Beginning"
Martha Munizzi – "New Season"

**Bringing in the Harvest**
Galatians 3:26, Ephesians 3:17, Ephesians 5:6, 2 Corinthians 5:19, 1 Corinthians 15:24, Galatians 5:24, Acts 2:24, Ephesians 2:1, 1 Peter 2:24

## Week 37

### DON'T BE ANXIOUS FOR ANYTHING

**Morning Glory Devotion**
"Do not be anxious about anything, but in every situation, by prayer and petition, with thanksgiving, present your requests to God." (Philippians 4:6)

**Growing in God's Word**
I learned a very valuable lesson about being anxious for nothing and making my requests known to God while visiting with my daughters who live in Texas. I had plenty of motherly advice to give to them but, at that time, my youngest daughter was not very receptive, which caused tension between us.

The next morning, during my devotional time, I prayed and waited for God's guidance in how to minister to my daughter's needs in a way other than giving her unsolicited advice. As I waited, I heard the Holy Spirit speak to my heart, saying that she needed my help more than she needed my advice. My daughter is a single mother of three very young boys and works a full-time job, which gives her very little time to do household chores. I knew immediately where the help was most needed—the boys' bedroom and closet!

The closet, where the most work was required, was my starting point. I folded and hung piles and piles of clothes that appeared to be as high as a mountain. After the fourth hour of working in the closet I took a step back and said, "Lord, I'm feeling very overwhelmed, and the closet still appears to be untouched."

The Holy Spirit revealed to me that this is how my daughter feels every day! I said, "Wow! God, thank you for showing me her need. I now understand!" I got a burst of new energy and completed the boy's closet and the laundry before my daughter returned home from work.

When she walked through the door and saw the obvious changes, she looked at me with tears in her eyes and said, "Mom, this is the best gift you could have given me. I was feeling so overwhelmed with the conditions of my house. I just didn't know where to start, but now I can maintain the work you have done for me."

We, as Christians, are called to be active believers, each day in every situation, showing others who Christ is whenever and wherever there may be a need that calls for our works— which, at times, can be more valuable than our words. Our words should be confirmed with the activation of our works that demonstrate God's grace and love, making Christ real in the lives of others and sharing that same grace God showed us.

**Digging Deeper into the Word** (Philippians 4:4-9)

DAY 1: Praise and Prayer Relieves Anxiety (Philippians 4:4-6)

- Praise God in every situation. (4v)
- Let your meed disposition be evident of God's presence in you. (5v)
- Don't let anxiety get the best of you. (v6a)
- Pray in every situation. (v6b)
- Prayer is the cure for anxiety. (v6c)

DAY 2: Our Peace in Christ (Phillipians 4:7)

- Peace surpasses our understanding. (v7a-b)
- Peace Guards our heart. (v7c)
- Peace of mind. (v7d)
- Peace in Jesus. (v7e)

DAY 3: Spiritual Mindset (Phillippians 4:8)
- Focus on what's True. (v8a)
- Focus on what's Honorable. (v8b)
- Focus on what's Holy and Pure. (v8c)
- Focus on what's Lovely. (v8d)
- Focus on God's Report. (v8e)
- Focus on Excellences. (v8f)
- Focus on Praiseworthy. (v8g)

DAY 4: Adhere to Godly Examples (Phillipians 4:9)
- Put into practice the Word of God that you've heard and been taught. (v9a)
- Emulate Godly behavior. (v9b)
- Implementation of Godly Practice brings the Peace of God in your life. (9c)

DAY 5: *Tilling the Heart*
Q1: How can praise and prayer help with anxiety?
Q2: How does the peace of God guard against anxiety?
Q3: What types of things that you can mediate on that can keep your mind at peace?
Q4: Describe how the peace of God empowers your daily life?
Q5: Describe how God's love can cure anxiety?

**Flowering in the Promises of God**
"For God hath not given us the spirit of fear; but of power, and of love and of a sound mind." (2 Timothy 1:7 KJV)

**Morning Glory Prayer**
*Heavenly Father, let peace be my guide today. Help me to complete every task without complaining and disputing. Let my words and my behavior demonstrate plainly your love and grace towards all people. Keep me blameless and by the power of your Holy Spirit let your light continue to shine in me for your glory. In Jesus' name I pray, Amen.*

**Tending to the Roots**
Phillippians 4:1-9

**Nourishing with Praise**
Youthful Praise – "Lord You're Mighty"
Hillsong – "You Are, You Are, Lord"
Lecresia Campbell & Faith Singers – "I'm In His Safety"
Meredith Andrews – "Soar"
Matt Maher – "Deliverer"

**Bringing in the Harvest**
Psalm 51:15, Pasalm 55:22, Poverbs 3:5-6, Matthew 6:25-33,
Luke 12:22, Romans 15:33, Romans 16:20, 1 Thessalonians
5:23, 1 Corinthians 14:33, 1 Peter 5:7, Colossians 3:15

# Week 38

## NO HARM WILL COME TO YOU

**Morning Glory Devotion**
"Because he loves me," says the LORD, "I will rescue him; I will protect him, for he acknowledges my name. He will call on me, and I will answer him; I will be with him in trouble, I will deliver him and honor him." (Psalms 91:14-15)

**Growing in God's Word**
Many years ago, I had a dream that I was walking beside a beautiful, flowing, crystal-clear stream on a peaceful, cool summer day. I was in the presence of God. I heard his voice ask me, "What do want from me, daughter?" I lifted my left palm up and pointed to it, and then answered Him, "Father, never lose me out of your care, always keep me safe in the palm of your hand. Don't let anything take me from you, not even myself." I begin to cry and sing praises to Him so loudly in my dream that I woke myself. I rose from my bed in continuous praise to Him. My heart was so full of admiration. That's when I realized I had fallen deeply in love with God.

God's word is my blessed assurance; it brings peace to my soul and fills my heart with His confirming love. God has promised to keep me safely in the palm of His hand. I've anchored myself in God's sacred place. In times of trouble, you can proclaim in Jesus' name, "What can snatch me out of my Father's hand?" What blessed assurance we have in God to know His divine protection will overpower all evil and keep us safely in His sacred place. O how I love God.

**Digging Deeper into the Word** (Psalms 91:1-16)

DAY 1: Hidden in God (Psalms 91:1-6)

- My sacred place is in God. (v1)
- My shelter is in Him. (v2)
- He is my deliverer. (v3)
- He is my Divine defense. (v4)
- I fear no evil. (v5)
- No deadly sickness shall come my way. (v6)

DAY 2: Protection from All Harm (Psalms 91:7-10)

- We will face destruction and dangers but remain unharmed. (v7)
- The righteous will witness the destruction of their enemies. (v8)
- We can dwell in the presence of the Most-High. (v9)
- God preserves us. (v10)

DAY 3: Divine Guardianship (Psalms 91:11-13)

- God gives us angelic protection. (v11)
- Angels shall provide safety from all dangers. (v12)
- They will overpower our enemies. (v13)

DAY 4: God Honors Our Love (Psalms 91:14-16)

- God responds to our devotion to Him. (v14)
- God responds to our prayer. (v15a)
- God stands with us in our time of troubles; He honors us with victory. (v15b)
- God gives abundance through Salvation. (v16)

DAY 5: *Tilling the Heart*

Q1: When did your love for God change to being *in love* with Him?

Q2: How would you describe your relationship with God?Q3: How has God delivered you from of danger?

Q4: What is the meaning of unconditional love to you?

Q5: When have you felt the presence of God and how did it feel?

**Flowering in the Promises of God**
"I have given you authority to trample on snakes and scorpions and to overcome all the power of the enemy; nothing will harm you." (Luke 10:19)

**Morning Glory Prayer**
*Heavenly Father, you have delivered me from all of my enemies with honor and victory. You have been attentive to all of my prayers when I call on you in my times of troubles, and you have protected me. I thank you, Lord, for life more abundant through Christ. I will abide in your love; I will trust in your Word, and I will honor you with my love all the days of my life. In Jesus' name I pray, Amen.*

**Tending to the Roots**
Psalms 91:1-16

**Nourishing with Praise**
Chris Tomlin – "Jesus Loves Me"
Shane & Shane, The Worship Initiative – "You Are My King (Amazing Love)"
Israel Houghton – "Chasing Me Down"
David Crowder – "How He Loves"
Israel Houghton – "My Tribute Medley"

**Bringing in the Harvest**
Psalms 17:8, Psalms 18:2, 2 Chronicles 20:9, Isaiah 51:16, Psalms 27:1, Psalms 58:10, Proverbs 12:21, Luke 4:10

## Week 39

TALKING WITH THE FATHER

**Morning Glory Devotion**
"For if you forgive men when they sin against you, your heavenly Father will also forgive you. But if you do not forgive men their sins, your Father will not forgive your sins." (Matthew 6:14-15)

**Growing in God's Word**
When worldly chatter and all its evil reports of senseless killings, mass shootings, crimes against the innocent, and the denouncing of God daily has consumed me, I pray the Lord's Prayer. The Lord's Prayer delivers protection, guidance, provision, forgiveness, and the power of God's will to be done on Earth as it is in Heaven. The Lord's Prayer restores my peace. Try using the Lord's Prayer when you are feeling overwhelmed with worldly chatter, you will find comfort in Him.

"Our Father which art in heaven, hallowed be thy name.
Thy kingdom come,
Thy will be done in earth, as it is in heaven.
Give us this day our daily bread.
And forgive us our debts, as we forgive our debtors.
And lead us not into temptation, but deliver us from evil.
For thine is the kingdom, and the power, and the glory, forever."
(Matthew 6:9-13, KJV)

In closing of my prayer, I say: *Father, I enter into my secret place and I pray in faith because you know the concerns and needs of my heart that I cannot convey, and I know you will rescue me from this attack of the enemy and give me rest from my wea-*

*riness. So, I exchange my will for your perfect will to be done. I thank you in advance for answering my prayer. In Jesus' name, I pray, Amen.*

**Digging Deeper into the Word** (Matthew 6:5-15)

DAY 1: Jesus' Instructions on Praying (Matthew 6:5-7)
- Pray with a sincere heart. (v5a)
- Do not pray to be seen and heard. (v5b)
- Do not seek public recognition for your reward. (v5c)
- Enter into a secret place for devotion. (v6a)
- What's done in secret God will reward publicly. (v6b)
- Pray in faith. (v7)

DAY 2: The Father Knows (Matthew 6:8-10)
- Don't imitate how hypocrites pray. (v8a)
- Prayer is not to inform God; He already knows our needs. (v8b)
- Jesus lays the foundation for the prayer of petition. (v9a)
- Acknowledge the Sovereign God. (v9b)
- Pray for God's righteousness and His will to be lived on the earth. (v10)

DAY 3: God's Provisions (Matthew 6:11-13)
- God provides our daily necessities of life. (v11)
- We must forgive to be forgiven. (v12)
- God will keep us from entering into trials and tests that we cannot endure. (v13a)
- God will rescue us from the power of Satan. (v13b)
- The Lord Almighty reigns with all power and honor forever. (v13c)

DAY 4: God's Forgiveness (Matthew 6:14-15)
- Walk in forgiveness to receive forgiveness. (v14)
- Unforgiving hearts lead to not being forgiven. (v15)

DAY 5: *Tilling the Heart*
Q1: How did Jesus instruct us to pray?

Q2: Why pray in secret?
Q3: What did Jesus tell us to avoid when praying?
Q4: How do you approach God in prayer? When you pray, what do you pray for?
Q5: What did Jesus teach about forgiveness?

## Flowering in the Promises of God
"And the prayer offered in faith will make the sick person well; the Lord will raise them up. If they have sinned, they will be forgiven." (James 5:15)

## Morning Glory Prayer
*Heavenly Father, may my prayers and my praise be acceptable and pleasing to your ears. I pray my heart reveals my sincere devotion and humbleness to you. Filter my words to line-up with your perfect will. Lord, help me to always walk in forgiveness so I may be able to receive your forgiveness. Today, I pray your will be done in me and on the earth as it is in heaven. In Jesus' name I pray, Amen.*

## Tending to the Roots
Matthew 6:5-15

## Nourishing with Praise
Brilliance – "Brother"
Elevation Worship – "Here as In Heaven"
Bethel Music – "Our Father"
Hillary Scott – "Thy Will"
Alisa Turner – "My Prayer for You"

## Bringing in the Harvest
Luke 18:11, Isaiah 26:20, 1 Kings 18:26, Luke 12:30, Luke 11:2, Acts 21:14, Isaiah 33:16, Ephesians 1:7, 2 Timothy 4:18, 2 Peter 2:9

## Week 40

### CHEERFUL GIVER

**Morning Glory Devotion**

"You will be enriched in every way so that you can be generous on every occasion, and through us your generosity will result in thanksgiving to God. This service that you perform is not only supplying the needs of the Lord's people but is also overflowing in many expressions of thanks to God." (2 Corinthians 9:11-12)

**Growing in God's Word**

After many years, my heart still overflows with gratitude toward those many people, known and unknown, who helped me and my children in our time of need, aiding us with money, food, clothing, car maintenance, words of encouragement, and prayers for financial blessings and security.

Many times, I received charity without request from those who were acting out of obedience to the promptings of the Holy Spirit concerning my needs, giving me hope, knowing that God heard my prayers and saw the struggles I endured, confirming that these struggles were temporary and that they would pass . . . and they did!

The genuine good will of my brothers and sisters in Christ had a great impact on me, and their expressions of loving-kindness through Christ Jesus and their humbleness toward me preserved my dignity. I continue to pray for the village of people who helped me in my time of need. I pray for them that God's bountiful grace will cover them—that they may lack nothing, always prospering financially, in health and spirit, and that their souls will always be satisfied with the everlasting riches and love of God.

**Digging Deeper in the Word** (2 Corinthian 9:6-15)


DAY 1: The Act of Generous Giving (2 Corinthians 9:6-9)
- You will receive in accordance to your giving. (v6)
- Give purposefully. (v7a)
- Don't give out of pressure or protesting or out of impulse. (v7b)
- God loves a cheerful giver who brings their offerings out of admiration. (v7c)
- God rewards a cheerful giver with abundance of grace. (v8a)
- A cheerful giver lacks nothing and prospers in all good works. (v8b)
- A cheerful giver obeys God's Word, giving charity freely to those without. (v9a)
- A cheerful giver's righteousness remains forever. (v9b)


DAY 2: Abundance of God's Blessings (2 Corinthians 9:10-11)
- We reap what we sow. (v10)
- Give thanks to God for your abundant living. (v11)


DAY 3: Praise and Admiration for God's Bountiful Blessings (2 Corinthians 9:12-13)
- Our charitable service that meets the needs of others glorifies God. (v12)
- Your declaration of Christ is demonstrated in your service to others. (v13)


DAY 4: Blessings Reciprocated: "Benefactor and the Giver" (2 Corinthians 9:14-15)
- The receiver offers prayers in thanks for the obedience of the cheerful giver. (v14)
- All gratitude is given to God for His gift of Christ Jesus our Lord and Savior. (v15)


DAY 5: *Tilling the Heart*
Q1: What does giving sparely or grudgingly mean?
Q2: What are your expectations of receiving back when giving to others? Why or why not?

Q3: How do you give differently when prompted by the Holy Spirit?

Q4: What are some of the different ways you can give?

Q5: When have you ever been blessed with a gift of charity that was a need only God could have inspired the giver to give? Or, have you been the giver? What was the situation and how did you respond?

**Flowering in the Promises of God**
"Give generously to him and do so without a grudging heart; then because of this the LORD your God will bless you in all your work and in everything you put your hand to." (Deuteronomy 15:10)

**Morning Glory Prayer**
*Heavenly Father, bless the cheerful giver—those who are willing and obedient to do your service of charity with joy according to your Word, serving with a humble heart. Lord, grant abundant blessings to the giver for their good works done to your glory. Today, my thankfulness overflows to you for your provisions that are all-sufficient to those who declare you to be their Lord and Savior. In Jesus' name, I pray. Amen.*

**Tending to the Roots**
2 Corinthians 9:6-15

**Nourishing with Praise**
Jesus Culture, Chris McClarney – "Everything and Nothing Less"
Robin Mark – "Blessed Be Your Name"
Sidewalk Prophets – "Come to the Table"
Travis Green (Amazing Worship) – "Made A Way"
Shana Wilson – "Give Me You"

**Bringing in the Harvest**
Proverbs 11:24, 1 Chronicles 29:17, Ephesians 3:20, Psalms 112:9, Hosea 10:12, 1 Corinthians 1:5, 2 Corinthians 8:14, Matthew 9:8, Romans 5:15

## Week 41

### KNOW GOD'S WORD FOR YOURSELF

**Morning Glory Devotion**
"Do not be misled: 'Bad company corrupts good character.'
Come back to your senses as you ought, and stop sinning; for
there are some who are ignorant of God—I say this to your
shame." (1 Corinthians 15:33-34)

**Growing in God's Word**
My thoughts were held captive by the Holy Spirit as I wrote this
devotion. I began to think of the many times God has delivered
me from deceit and danger even when I was not in compliance
with His Word. Because I am His child the promptings of the
Holy Spirit warn me when I am in error allowing me to repent
and get back in right standing with God.

There may be times when God will send you a
trustworthy, mature God-fearing Christian who you will accept
correction and guidance from when in error of God's Word.
This is not the time to be offended or prideful. This is a learning
moment; God's mercy is protecting you from being deceived or
mislead by erroneous beliefs or false doctrines that may cause
you to walk in error, which could lead to you jeopardizing your
life.

I grew up in a faith that forbids divorce for any
reason. Even though my marriage almost led to my death, I
was not willing to divorce and I kept myself and my children in
an abusive situation for many years. When I finally had enough
of the abuse and was no longer willing to accept it, I prayed for
safe passage out. I know without a doubt it was God who
intervened on my behalf. I eventually left that church, but it

wasn't until years later when I began to learn through the study of God's Word and godly mentors the true meaning of perfect love and God's ordained purpose and commands for marriage.

Don't let lack of knowledge of God's Word cause you to be deceived or live in error. Study, learn, pray, and seek God for understanding and biblical truths. Confirm correction and godly counsel through God's Word.

**Digging Deeper into the Word** (1 Corinthians 15:20-34)

DAY 1: Sin Conquered by the Resurrection of Christ (1 Corinthians 15: 20-24)
- Christ's resurrection gives hope for salvation. (v20)
- The consequence of original sin is that all men are condemned to death, but through the death, burial, and resurrection of Christ Jesus we were redeemed. (v21-22)
- Christ is coming again. (v23)
- Jesus Christ has all authority over evil and delivers the keys of life, death, and hell to God. (v24)

DAY 2: Christ's Triumph Over Evil (1 Corinthians 15: 25-28)
- Christ tramples the enemy under His feet. (v25)
- Christ defeats death. (v26)
- Christ has absolute authority over everything on the earth, beneath the earth, and in the heavenly realm. (v27-28)

DAY 3: Believers' Reassurance in Christ (1 Corinthians 15: 29-31)
- The destination of eternal life is determined by your belief in Christ. (v29-30)
- Though I suffer daily in the flesh, I live daily through Christ. (v31)

DAY 4: Lacking Understanding of God's Word (1 Corinthians 15: 32-34)
- If the resurrection of Christ is false, then the sufferings for His name's sake are in vain. (v32)

- Do not be misled by communication of unbelief by those who deny resurrection. (v33)
- Do not depart from the truth or be misled by other erroneous doctrines that deny the resurrection. (v34)

DAY 5: *Tilling the Heart*
Q1: Have you ever been misled by someone's belief because of lack of knowledge of God's Word? Why or why not?
Q2: How do you receive correction from another brother or sister in Christ?
Q3: Have you ever corrected anyone based on biblical principles and truths? Why or why not?
Q4: How do you check your understanding and knowledge of God's Word to ensure that you are not being deceived?
Q5: How would you explain the different meanings between correction and rebuke?

**Flowering in the Promises of God**
"Here is a trustworthy saying: If we died with him, we will also live with him." (2 Timothy 2:11)

**Morning Glory Prayer**
*Heavenly Father, where I lack knowledge and understanding of your Word, lead me to your truths and give me discernment to recognize false teachings and the evil chatter of this world. If I have error in your Word, please remove the scales from my eyes so I may see my misleading actions. Today I'm running back to your saving grace with a repentant heart. In Jesus' name, I pray. Amen.*

**Tending to the Roots**
1 Corinthians 15:20-34

**Nourishing with Praise**
Brenton Brown – "Word of God"

Jeremy Camp – "Living Word"
MercyMe – "Word of God Speak"
Maurice Brown – "I Am Healed by the Word of God"
Casting Crowns – "Voice of Truth"

**Bringing in the Harvest**
1 Peter 1:3, Romans 5:12, Romans 5:14, Revelation 1:5, Daniel 7:14, Psalms 110:1, 2 Timothy 1:10, Matthew 11:27, Philippians 3:21, 2 Corinthians 11:26

## Week 42

### GOD'S GRACE CONSUMES OUR AFFLICTIONS

**Morning Glory Devotion**
"We are hard pressed on every side, but not crushed; perplexed, but not in despair; persecuted, but not abandoned; struck down, but not destroyed. So we fix our eyes not on what is seen, but on what is unseen, since what is seen is temporary, but what is unseen is eternal." (2 Corinthians 4:8-9, 18)

**Growing in God's Word**
The horrific abuse I had suffered in my marriage shattered my self-worth, but God's love and grace freed me emotionally and physically, giving me the fortitude to share my testimony of God's mighty acts in my life with other women who have been abused in the past or are currently being abused.

I have come to realize that it was God's love and His Grace interceding on my behalf that protected me through the many adversities and disappointments that came my way.
Since those abusive times in my life, I have grown a lot through the knowledge of God. It's been with God's grace that I have been able to grow spiritually to the point where I was able to forgive my abuser.

The afflictions of abuse nearly destroyed me, but it was by the living power of God's grace that I'm healed of all the injuries and shame. And now, I'm not afraid to show my battle scars of victory and to give my testimony of God's deliverance. It was the overflow of God's grace that has given me the strength and hope to move forward with life.

His grace can bring you through any challenge you face in life, so turn to Him for guidance and protection. There is nothing you will face that He can't bring you through.

**Digging Deeper in the Word**   2 Corinthians 4:1-18

DAY 1: The Light of Gospel Enlightens the Mind (2 Corinthians 4:1-6)
- We are appointed by God's Mercy to minister the Gospel. (v1)
- We are to demonstrate the truth of the Gospel. (v2)
- The Gospel is hidden to those who are lost. (v3)
- The light of the Gospel is unable to penetrate the worldly mind. (v4)
- Jesus preached the Gospel. (v5)
- The knowledge of Jesus Christ penetrates a receiving heart. (v6)

DAY 2: The Knowledge of Christ Is the Power of God to Preserve Us (2 Corinthians 4:7-10)
- The power of God is in earthly vessels. (v7)
- The knowledge and the power of Christ consumes our worries. (v8)
- The power of God is our protection during our persecution. (v9)
- The power of God helps us to manifest Christ in our lives. (v10)

DAY 3: The Benefits of Christ Living in Us (2 Corinthians 4:11-15)
- Christ is manifested in us. (v11)
- The death, burial, and the resurrection of Christ gives life. (v12)
- There is power in the spoken Word of Christ. (v13)
- The resurrection power dwells within us. (v14)
- The overflowing grace and the power of God allows our afflictions to be used for God's glory. (v15)

DAY 4: Body and Soul (2 Corinthians 4:16-18)
- We are strengthened by the grace of God. (v16a)
- Denying the Outward Man allows for the manifestation of Christ in our flesh. (v16b)
- Our Inward Man—our soul—is renewed daily by the light of Christ in our lives. (v16c)

- Our present burdens can't be compared to God's exceeding glory. (v17)
- Our focus is not on the temporary things of this world but on the eternal things that have been revealed by the knowledge and power of Christ. (v18)

DAY 5: *Tilling the Heart*
Q1: What affliction(s) have you suffered that have been covered and are being sustained by God's grace?
Q2: What scriptures can you use to define Inward Man?
Q3: What scriptures can you use to define Outward Man?
Q4: What is the difference between the seen temporal and the unseen eternal?
Q5: How is the power of God manifested in your life?

## Flowering in the Promises of God

"The righteous person may have many troubles, but the Lord delivers him from them all." (Psalms 34:19)

## Morning Glory Prayer

*Heavenly Father, the God of all surpassing power, my present burdens cannot be compared to the promises of Your abounding grace toward me. I fix my eyes not on life's afflictions and sufferings but on Gods' grace where all my strength and power to endure comes from. I will not lose heart because it's all working for my good day-to-day. In Jesus' name, I pray. Amen.*

## Tending to the Roots
2 Corinthians 4:1-18

## Nourishing with Praise
Hillsong Worship – "Desert Song"
Martha Munizzi – "Because of Who You Are"
Brooklyn Tabernacle Choir – "Hallelujah Anyhow"
Tasha Cobbs – "Break Every Chain"

Mandisa – "What Scars Are For"

**Bringing in the Harvest**
Acts 26:18, 1 Corinthians 2:5, Proverbs 24:16, Romans 6:5, Ro-mans 6:8, Psalms 116:10, Acts 2:24, Romans 8:28, Isaiah 40:29, Romans 8:18

# Week 43

## PUTTING ON CHRIST JESUS

**Morning Glory Devotion**
"Stand firm then, with the belt of truth buckled around your waist, with the breastplate of righteousness in place, and with your feet fitted with the readiness that comes from the gospel of peace." (Ephesians 6:14-15)

**Growing in God's Word**
As I walked away from the podium, the audience stood to their feet and applauded my testimony that I shared with them about my physical abuse and how God's mighty acts delivered me.

I returned to my seat in the conference room with a sense of victory for God. But this victory fell under sudden attack by evil spirits of defiance and offense trying to discredit my testimony by calling me a fake Christian.

I was unaware at that moment and unprepared for this sudden spiritual attack that greeted me soon after speaking. I had to make a decision: Was I going to react to this defiant spirit and allow it to act contrary to my testimony about forgiveness and God's love? Was I willing to allow my stance to steal the testimony of God's power and healing grace over my life.

No, not so, I chose to act with love and to continue to stand on biblical truths. I remained strengthened in God's power that dwelled within me. I had prepared myself prior to speaking, in prayer, in study, and putting on Jesus Christ. So, as a representative of God I was able to continue to stand boldly and to share the gospel in peace with all truths. And the power of the spoken Word of God protected me and set the captive free from the strongholds of the enemy. The plans of the evil spirits for ruining my testimony and to destroy this precious soul were defeated by God's saving grace.

**Digging Deeper in the Word** (Ephesians 6:10-20)

DAY 1: Spiritual Battle Preparation (Ephesians 6:10-12)
- Remain in the spiritual strength through God's power that dwells within you. (v10)
- Put on the Lord Jesus Christ completely and His mighty power. (v11a)
- Be prepared for the prince of evil spirit's plans for ruining the souls of men. (v11b)
- Our battle of life is not with men but with a world overshadowed by sin, by spiritual hosts of wickedness and evil spirits under the orders of the devil residing in the regions of the air. (v12)

DAY 2: Spiritual Watchfulness: Be on Guard, Stand Your Ground (Ephesians 6:13)
- Suit up with the armor of God. (v13a)
- Evil will launch an offensive attack. (v13b)
- Stand your ground. (v13c)
- Once all the spiritual preparation has been done, take the defensive fighting posture (dig in) and stand your ground. (v13d)

DAY 3: Spiritual Battle Required Equipment (Ephesians 6:14-17)
- Spiritual agility of the mind is strengthened by the truths of God's Word. (v14a)
- The breastplate of righteousness offers protection for a righteous heart. (v14b)
- The messenger of God prepares and shares the Gospel of peace. (v15)
- Standing on the Word of God helps you guard against the temptation of sin and sudden attacks from the enemy. (v16)
- There is power in the spoken Word of God. (v17)

DAY 4: The Necessities of Prayer (Ephesians 6:18-20)
- Always pray, interceding for our sisters and brothers in Christ Jesus. (v18)
- Intercede in prayer for all messengers of the Gospel, speak with boldness to make known the Gospel of Christ to everyone. (v19-20)

DAY 5: *Tilling the Heart*
Q1: What spiritual battle equipment is needed for a spiritual war?
Q2: What is the Breastplate of Righteousness?
Q3: What is the Shield of Faith?
Q4: Why should you pray without ceasing?
Q5: What is intercessory prayer?

**Flowering in the Promises of God**
"For though we live in the world, we do not wage war as the world does. The weapons we fight with are not the weapons of the world. On the contrary, they have divine power to demolish strongholds. We demolish arguments and every pretension that sets itself up against the knowledge of God, and we take captive every thought to make it obedient to Christ." (2 Corinthians 10:3-5)

"The God of peace will soon crush Satan under your feet. The grace of our Lord Jesus be with you." (Romans 16:20)

**Morning Glory Prayer**
*Heavenly Father, You have prepared me with the weaponry I need to be victorious when adversity comes. I stand firm with the belt of truth buckled around my waist and covered by the breastplate of righteousness. I boldly pray, interceding on behalf of my sisters and brothers in Christ Jesus, with my feet ready to share the Gospel of peace. Today the power of God's Word strengthens me; I am an overcomer. In Jesus' name, I pray. Amen.*

**Tending to the Roots**
Ephesians 6: 10-20

**Nourishing with Praise**
Shirley Caesar – "Armor of God"
Fred Hammond – "No Weapon Formed Against Me"
Kurt Carr – "Oh, My Soul Loves Jesus"
CeCe Winans – "Waging War"
Yolanda Adams – "The Battle Is the Lord's"
Youthful Praise – "Lord You're Mighty"

**Bringing in the Harvest**
2 Timothy 2:1, Romans 13:12, Colossians 1:13, James 4:7, Isaiah
59:17, Isaiah 52:7, Psalms 7:13, Hebrews 4:12

# Week 44

CHRIST OUR DEFENDER

**Morning Glory Devotion**
"If we confess our sins, He is faithful and just and will forgive us our sins and purify us from all unrighteousness." (1 John 1:9)

**Growing in God's Word**
In our sinful state, we have to understand the importance of confessing our sins, which allows us to come out of darkness and return to the marvelous light of Christ, the Living Word.

I was baptized as a young girl, and I can still remember clearly the joy and freedom I experienced in the Lord and my zeal to share the good news of Jesus Christ with everyone I came in contact with. I wanted them to have what I felt.

Our confession works the same way, cleansing us from guilt and condemnation and releasing us to start anew, having zeal to continue to seek and grow in Christ. Sharing the Word of God in fellowship with others and proclaiming the mighty power of God's work in our lives brings that fresh faith to us every day. Whether you are a new Christian or have many years of faith behind you, each day should fill you with the joy of being in Christ and inspire you to share that gift with every person you meet. If you are feeling stagnant in your faith, pray for the Holy Spirit to fill you with renewed excitement for the Gospel.

**Digging Deeper in the Word** (1 John 1:1-10)

DAY 1: What Was Heard, Seen, and Touched by the Word (1 John 1: 1-4)
- The Word became life. (v1a)
- God's spoken Word was heard. (v1b)

- The Word made flesh was seen by all. (v1c)
- Our eyes were opened to the manifestation of the Word. (v1d)
- All were touched by the Word of life. (v1e)
- The believers bear witness of the Word made flesh and proclaim Jesus to all. (v2)
- We can now fellowship with "What we have Seen, Heard, and Touched." (v3)
- Fellowshipping with the manifested Word of God fulfills our joy. (v4)

DAY 2: The Light Reveled (1 John 1:5-6)
- The Gospel declares the light. (v5a)
- God is that light. (v5b)
- The light voids out darkness. (v5c)
- Let your conversation and actions line-up with the truth of the God's Word. (v6)

DAY 3: Living in the Light (1 John 1:7-8)
- Fellowship with Christ and one another. (v7a)
- Fellowshipping in the salvation of Christ purifies us from all sins. (v7b)
- We deceive ourselves when we fail to acknowledge our sins. (v8)

DAY 4: Confessions Lead to Salvation (1 John 1:9-10)
- Confession leads to our deliverance. (v9a)
- We have been justified through Christ: the blood washes us clean of all of our sins. (v9b)
- Our denial of sin denies the power of God working in our lives. (v10)

DAY 5: *Tilling the Heart*
Q1: What description in the text is used to describe Christ?
Q2: How would you explain the statement, "What is seen, heard, and touched"?
Q3: How do we deceive ourselves by denying our sins?
Q4: How do you define fellowship?
Q5: How do you fellowship with Christ and others?

## Flowering in the Promises of God

"As for you, see that what you have heard from the beginning remains in you. If it does, you also will remain in the Son and in the Father. And this is what he promised us—eternal life." (1 John 2:24-25)

## Morning Glory Prayer

*Heavenly Father, today I confess that I have not always been obedient to what you have required of me through your Word. I'm thankful for your faithfulness in forgiving me for all of my unrighteousness. Lord, help me to continue following the light of your Word so that I may attain all of the promises that you have guaranteed us. In Jesus' name, I pray. Amen.*

## Tending to the Roots

1 John 1:1-10

## Nourishing with Praise

Matt Maher – "Your Love Defends Me"
Jessica Di Giovanni – "Defend Us"
Eddie James – "Breakthrough"
Tamela Mann – "Change Me"
Tramaine Hawkins – "Changed"

## Bringing in the Harvest

2 Timothy 2:1, Romans 13:12, Colossians 1:13, James 4:7, Isaiah 59:17, Isaiah 52:7, Psalms 7:13, Hebrews 4:12

# Week 45

## GOD'S MIGHTY WORKS

**Moring Glory Devotion**
"He has performed mighty deeds with his arm; he has scattered those who are proud in their inmost thoughts." (Luke 1:51)

**Growing in God's Word**
Daily we see and hear about the mighty works of God being performed in the world, which are called miracles—lives being saved from horrific disasters of earthquakes, floods, and fires; being protected from sudden attacks of mass shootings and bombings; escaping near-fatal accidents with only scratches; the survival of a child being born two months early; or a life being saved by the deed of a Good Samaritan.

But how often do we acknowledge God's mighty acts of touching our lives every morning with life? Do we magnify and praise His name for giving us new mercies and grace each morning? Do we humble ourselves unto God for giving us another chance to repent and to seek the forgiveness of others?

The blessing of life is a miracle of God's mighty work, giving us a new day with the ability to praise Him. Having a new opportunity to fulfill God's purpose and share with others the greatness of His mercy and love is a miracle for which we should praise God. Each day of life isn't by luck; it is God's blessing and favor bestowed upon us. How are you going to use the gift of life today?

**Digging Deeper in the Word** (Luke 1: 46–55)

DAY 1: Mother of God (Luke 1:46-48)
- From the depths of Mary's soul, she magnified the Lord. (v46)

- Mary's spirit acknowledges our LORD and savior with praises. (v47)
- She is chosen because of her humility. (v48a)
- Her name shall be called blessed through all generations. (v48b)

DAY 2: God Uses the Humble in a Mighty Way (Luke 1:49-51)
- We are selected for God's mighty works. (v49)
- The favor of God is upon those who revere Him. (v50)
- The mighty acts of God are demonstrated through His touch. (v51a)
- God resists the proud. (v51b)

DAY 3: The Mighty Works of God Being Performed Through Humility (Luke 1:52-54)
- God exalts the humble. (v52)
- God satisfies those who are hungry for His Word. (v53a)
- Those who do not hunger or thirst are empty. (v53b)
- God has shown His great mercy to His people. (v54)

DAY 4: The Chosen (Luke 1:55)
- God's mercy extends to all the generations of Abraham seed. (v55)

DAY 5: *Tilling the Heart*
Q1: What miracles have you witnessed?
Q2: How would you describe Mercy?
Q3: What does it mean to have the fear of the LORD?
Q4: Why is it important to be humble?
Q5: What is a miracle of God that was demonstrated in your life?

**Flowering in the Promises of God**
"Very truly I tell you, whoever believes in me will do the works I have been doing, and they will do even greater things than these, because I am going to the Father." (John 14:12)

**Morning Glory Prayer**

*Heavenly Father, today, I cast down any pride that dwells with-in me that interferes with my relationship with You. I humbly submit myself to you, the one who has performed mighty works that no man can take credit for, and I thank you for extending your mercy to the world through Jesus Christ. In Jesus' name I pray. Amen.*

**Tending to the Roots**
Luke 1:46-55

**Nourishing with Praise**
Francesca Battistelli – "Giants Fall"
Austin & Lindsey Adamec – "Maker of Miracles"
Chris McClarney – "God of Miracles"
Marvin Sapp – "You Are God Alone"
Hezekiah Walker - "God Favored Me"
Charles Jenkins – "My God Is Awesome"

**Bringing in the Harvest** Psalms 34:2, Habakkuk 3:18, Psalms 138:6, Psalms 103:17, Psalms 98:1, Job 5:11, Psalms 107:9, Genesis 17:7

# Week 46

## GOD'S IMITATORS: THE LIGHT OF THE WORLD

**Morning Glory Devotion**
"Follow God's example, therefore, as dearly loved children and walk in the way of love, just as Christ loved us and gave himself up for us as a fragrant offering and sacrifice to God." (Ephesians 5:1-2)

**Growing in God's Word**
My two daughters are one year apart in age. As little girls, they were inseparable. My older daughter, Ebony, was experiencing vision problems at the age of five, which required her to wear glasses. The very same week Ebony got her glasses, I received a phone call from my younger daughter's teacher informing me that Jasmine was complaining that she was unable to see the chalkboard at all. The teacher went on to explain that, based on her difficulties in seeing the chalkboard, she moved Jasmine to the front of the classroom. However, my sweet little girl still insisted that she could not see at all, and because of this she was not able to do her school work.

I immediately took Jasmine to the optometrist to get an eye exam. This was her first time visiting an eye doctor and I explained to the doctor the reason we were there. The doctor lifted little Jasmine up and placed her in the exam chair. He asked her a series of questions to which she gave the same answers as she did with her teacher, saying she couldn't see at all.

During the examination, the doctor pointed to the bottom line of the eye chart and asked Jasmine, "Tell me, what do you see on this line?" Jasmine replied, "I cannot see at all," so the doctor continued moving up to the next line and repeating the same question. This went on until the doctor reached the top of the eye chart. At this point I became frustrated and concerned. I interrupted the examination and firmly said to Jasmine, "What do you mean you can't see at all? Are you blind?" The doctor politely asked me to go wait in the waiting room for just a moment. I agreed and left the room. Moments later, the doctor and my little Jasmine came walking out of the room; she had a lollipop in her hand and was smiling. The doctor asked to see me in his office and asked if anyone in the house had gotten glasses recently.

I told him my oldest daughter had gotten her glasses that week. He smiled and said, "I understand now what's going on." He explained that when he placed a pair of non-prescription glasses on Jasmine's eyes, she was able to see perfectly. Jasmine just wanted glasses like her big sister!

Just like Jasmine's bond of love with her big sister made her want to be like her, we, as Christians, should have that same kind of devotion to Christ, desiring to be just like Him and become rooted in His Word. We should live by God's truths and the fruit of the Spirit that causes the light of our good works to shine before men, casting a spiritual radiance of our love for God.

**Digging Deeper in the Word** (Ephesians 5:1-21)

DAY 1: The Children of God Imitate Christ (Ephesians 5:1-5)
- Live in the light of Christ. (v1a)
- Live a life of love. (v1b)
- Demonstrate the same love as Christ demonstrated for us. (v2)
- Let there be no un-Christ-like behavior in relationships. (v3)
- Let there be no un-Christ-like communication. (v4)
- No impure person shall enter into the kingdom of God. (v5)

DAY 2: Fellowshipping with the Light Produces Spiritual Fruit (Ephesians 5:6-12)
- Children of disobedience are deceived with vain words. (v6)
- Do not fellowship with children of disobedience. (v7)
- Continue to walk as children of light. (v8)
- Children of the light produce fruit that is acceptable and righteous to the Lord. (v9-10)
- The children of light expose works of darkness and things done in secret. (v11-12)

DAY 3: The Light Penetrates Darkness (Ephesians 5:13-17)
- Evil cannot masquerade in the light. (v13)
- Spiritual awakening leads to salvation. (v14)
- Salvation leads to living in the light of Christ. (v15)
- Take every opportunity to let the light of Christ shine into a world of darkness. (v16)
- Know the will of God for your life. (v17)

DAY 4: Your Dedication, Devotion and Reverence unto the Lord (Ephesians 5:18-21)
- Exercise the spiritual fruit of self-control. (v18)
- Continue in worship, praise, and thanksgiving. (v19-20)
- Continue in service in humility. (v21)

DAY 5: *Tilling the Heart*
Q1: What does living a life of purity mean to you?
Q2: How has your spiritual life changed since you have accepted Christ?
Q3: How has your life encouraged someone else to accept Christ?
Q4: How would you explain your dedication, devotion, and reverence unto the Lord?
Q5: In what ways are you imitating God?

**Flowering in the Promises of God**
"But we all, with open face beholding as in a glass the glory of the Lord, are changed into the same image from glory to glory, even as by the Spirit of the Lord." (2 Corinthians 3:18 KJV)

**Morning Glory Prayer**
*Heavenly Father, I'm devoted to letting the light of Christ shine through me into a world of darkness. I pray that my life demonstrates self-control, purity, and brotherly love. Lord, guide me daily to live by your truths and by the fruit of the Spirit which causes me to imitate your good works that lead to spiritual awakening and salvation. Today, I'm letting my light shine for God's glory. In Jesus' name, I pray. Amen.*

**Tending to the Roots**
Ephesians 5:1-21

**Nourishing with Praise**
Hillsong-Glorious Ruins – "To Be Like You"
Clint Brown – "I Wanna Be More Like You, I Will Bless the Lord"
Elevation Worship – "Shine a Light"
Lauren Daigle – "Light of the World"

**Bringing in the Harvest**
Matthew 5:48, 2 Corinthians 2:14, Colossians 3:5, Ephesians 4:29, 1 Corinthians 6:9, Colossians 2:8, Acts 26:18, Galatians 5:22, Romans 12:2, John 3:20, Colossians 3:17

# Week 47

## A TIME AND A SEASON FOR EVERYTHING

**Morning Glory Devotion**
"I know that everything God does will endure forever; nothing can be added to it and nothing taken from it. God does it so that people will fear him." (Ecclesiastes 3:14)

**Growing in God's Word**
I have a picture hanging on a wall in my home that reads: *The One Thing That Remains Constant Is Change.*

I read it often to remind myself of the cycles and changes of life. It starts with birth and ends with death; but, in between, we are living. In our life experiences, we make good and bad choices and we must deal with the outcome of those choices. Birthdays come and go. Promises are made and broken. Relationships have different levels of commitment—some friendships last a lifetime and others only for a season; people fall in and out of love; sometimes we build families while others abandon them because of selfish desires. Human activities change constantly.

We cannot count on things in this life to stay the same because God's divine purpose is appointed and it will come to pass, which means change. But, God is good; He is perfect in all His ways. His Word endures forever. God's promises are yes and amen. God's will is perfect. God is the same yesterday, today, and forevermore! God's unconditional love for us will never change. God will never abandon us. God's attributes are everlasting, never changing. That is something we can count on.

## Digging Deeper in the Word (Ecclesiastes 3:1-17)

**DAY 1: Appointed Time for All Things (Ecclesiastes 3:1-8)**
- There is a chosen time for all human events on the earth. (v1)
- There is a chosen time for birth, dying, sowing, and weeding out. (v2)
- There is a chosen time for adversity, spiritual healing, breaking down, and building up. (v3)
- There is a chosen time for sadness, laugher, and celebration. (v4)
- There is a chosen time for letting go, restoring, rejection, and acceptance. (v5)
- There is a chosen time for increase, decrease, possession, giving away. (v6)
- There is a chosen time for separating, uniting, listening, and engaging. (v7)
- There is a chosen time for love, hate, war, and peace. (v8)

**DAY 2: The Fruits of Our Labor (Ecclesiastes 3:9-11)**
- We may wonder what we gain from our labor. (v9)
- God has expectations of men. (v10)
- Eternity cannot be earned through man's labor. (v11)

**DAY 3: The Gift of God: Life (Ecclesiastes 3:12-14)**
- Celebrate the goodness of life. (v12)
- Enjoy the fruits of our labor. (v13)
- The sovereignty of God is to be revered by men. (v14)

**DAY 4: The Season for Judgment (Ecclesiastes 3:15-17)**
- There is nothing new under the sun. (v15)
- Wickedness and righteousness exist under the sun. (v16)
- The works of the wicked and righteous shall be judged. (v17)

**DAY 5:** *Tilling the Heart*
Q1: How would you describe the season of life you are in now?
Q2: What are the benefits of your labor?
Q3: How do you show God your appreciation for life?

Q4: How will your works be judged? Why do you feel that way?
Q5: How do we maintain our happiness in a world of constant change?

**Flowering in the Promises of God**
"Jesus Christ is the same yesterday and today and forever." (Hebrews 13:8)

"I the Lord do not change. So you, the descendants of Jacob, are not destroyed." (Malachi 3:6)

**Morning Glory Prayer**
*Heavenly Father, I thank you for being an immutable God in a world of constant change. Thank you for your Holy Spirit that empowers me with your enduring peace, joy, and unconditional love that will sustain me in the changes of my life. In Jesus' name, I pray. Amen*

**Tending to the Roots**
Ecclesiastes 3:1-17

**Nourishing with Praise**
Tim Hughes – "Ecclesiastes"
Elevation Worship – "Unchanging God"
Jennifer Hudson – "Wonderful Change"
Chicago Mass Choir – "Hold to God's Unchanging Hand"
Michael Ketterer – "Seasons Change"

**Bringing in the Harvest**
Ecclesiastes 8:6, Hebrews 9:27, Hosea 6:1, Romans 12:15, Amos 5:13, Psalms 101:3, Ecclesiastes 1:3, Job 5:9, Genesis 18:25

# Week 48

## ANCHORED IN GOD'S WORD

**Morning Glory Devotion**

"Do not repay evil with evil or insult with insult. On the contrary, repay evil with blessing, because to this you were called so that you may inherit a blessing." (1 Peter 3:9)

**Growing in God's Word**

I listened intensely as he gave his testimony—this gentle and giving man sharing the story of his mother dying when he was a very young child and growing up with a father who did not acknowledge him. He was a motherless and fatherless child subjected to abuse only to find refuge in an old abandoned car. I thought, *How could he be so kind and giving, not holding back his love?*

He professed his hopelessness and his anger with God as a young boy. His rebellious stance didn't satisfy his unanswered questions, so he chose to overcome his obstacles of abandonment, abuse, and anger by seeking God for answers. In his pursuit of God, God met him right in his anguish and restored him through the many acts of kindness from his community and the many prayers prayed on his behalf. At age thirteen, God's Word and grace cracked and crumbled the hardness of his heart. At age fifteen, he accepted Jesus Christ as his Lord and Savior and was baptized, joining his local church. As he continued to build his relationship with God, he realized that it was God's love and grace that interceded on his behalf, protecting and providing for him in the times when there wasn't anyone else.

He decided not to live a life of retaliation and bitterness and instead to seek God and find his self-worth and his identity in Him. The Holy Spirit interceded on his behalf, giving him a Word that said, "He can do all things through Christ Jesus." This Word of God kept him anchored in the hope of God's promises concerning him.

It was God's Agape Love that enabled him to open his heart to receive love. Changing his anger to acceptance, fear to forgiveness, and loneliness for peace that only comes from God. Who do you pursue in times of adversities?

**Digging Deeper in the Word** (1 Peter 3:8-22)

DAY 1: Be a Doer of Good Works (1 Peter 3:8-11)
- Live peacefully with brotherly loving-kindness toward all. (v8)
- Don't exchange evil acts for evil, but choose to do good in order to receive blessings. (v9)
- Speak words of life not death. (v10)
- Choose to live a good life in peace without evil. (v11)

DAY 2: Rejoice in Well Doing (1 Peter 3:12-14)
- The work of the righteous God sees and he acts on their prayers. (v12a)
- The wrath of God is on those who disobey. (v12b)
- God protects those who follow after goodness. (v13)
- If the upright are persecuted for good works, great is their reward. (v14)

DAY 3: A Testimony that Glorifies God (1 Peter 3: 15-17)
- Worship and praise God in your sufferings. (v15a)
- In humility, let your testimony to men glorify God. (v15b)
- Let your conversation with those who persecute you be a testimony of Christ's goodness. (v16)
- Let your suffering be for the will of God and not for evil doing. (v17)

DAY 4: The Gift of the Holy Spirit through Salvation (1 Peter 3: 18-22)
- The finished work of Christ through His suffering brings salvation. (v18a)
- Sinners are justified through salvation. (v18b)
- Reconcile with God through the Holy Spirit. (v18c)
- Christ has the victory over Satan, the prince of darkness. (v19)
- God is long-suffering for His children. (v20)
- The power of baptism demonstrates the resurrection of Christ Jesus. (v21)
- All power is in His hands. (v22)

DAY 5: *Tilling the Heart*
Q1: What have you suffered for Christ's sake?
Q2: How do your conversations reflect Christ to those who are persecuting you?
Q3: How do you revere God in your trials?
Q4: What does water baptism symbolize?
Q5: How does your testimony give hope to others?

**Flowering in the Promises of God**
"And God is able to make all grace abound to you, so that in all things at all times, having all that you need, you will abound in every good work." (2 Corinthians 9:8)

**Morning Glory Prayer**
*Heavenly Father, you have never been absent from my life. It was me who stepped away from you. It's always been me who has fallen short in my obedience of your Word. It's always been me blaming you for the wrong acts done to me; it's always been me not willing to wait for your perfect will to be done. It's always been me changing constantly based on my feelings. But God, in spite of my insults and wrongdoings, I have learned that you have never changed at all. You've always been standing there with open arms to take me back in all my filth and cleanse me*

*through your divine grace, mercy, and love. Father, I repent for my wrong thinking and retaliation toward others and toward you. In Jesus' name, I pray. Amen.*

**Tending to the Roots**
1 Peter 3:8-22

**Nourishing with Praise**
Norman Hutchins – "God's Got a Blessing (with My Name on It)"
VaShawn Mitchell – "Turning Around for Me"
William McDowell – "Falling on My Knees"
Marvin Sapp – "Never Would've Made It"
Smokie Norful – "I Understand"
DeWayne Woods – "I Won't Be Afraid"

**Bringing in the Harvest**
Romans 12:16, Luke 6:28, Psalms 34:13, Psalms 34:14, Psalms 34:15-16, Proverbs 16:7, Matthew 5:10, Colossians 4:6, Hebrews 13:18, 1 Peter 1:6, Hebrews 10:10

## Week 49

### GOD QUALIFIES US FOR HIS SERVICE

**Morning Glory Devotion**
"I thank Christ Jesus our Lord, who has given me strength, that he considered me faithful, appointing me to his service." (1 Timothy 1:12)

**Growing in God's Word**
So many times, I've heard people say they'll go to church when they stop smoking, drinking, or partying. They believe they need to change their lives before they can give it to God or go to church.

This is not sound thinking. Only God can clean you up. When God chooses to use you, he wants you exactly as you are. He meets you where you are. God appeals to us to come to Him as we are. He qualifies the sinner for His service. The Bible teaches us that Jesus died on the cross while we all were still sinners and that He desires that no one should perish and go to Hell.

When you say yes to Jesus' salvation plan, submitting yourself to Him, the redemption of God's saving grace flows to you, covering your sins and purging you of the brokenness in your life. God heals you by filling in the cracks and chips of your broken vessel (your heart) with His unconditional love, patiently wooing you with His everlasting grace.

God has appointed you to be His representative to share with others about your transformation out of the darkness of sin into His marvelous light of salvation. God has exchanged your ashes for beautiful feet that carry God's Word.

**Digging Deeper in the Word** (1 Timothy 1:12-20)

DAY 1: The Call to Ministry (1 Timothy 1:12-14)
- God equips us for service. (v12)
- God shows mercy to the ignorant. (v13)
- Abundant grace is purposely given to the unbeliever. (v14)

DAY 2: Jesus Christ Salvation Plan Accessible to All (1 Timothy 1:15-16)
- Jesus' earthly mission was to bring salvation for all sinners. (v15)
- Mercy, grace, forgiveness, and eternal life are obtained through Christ. (v16)

DAY 3: The Accountability in Ministry (1 Timothy 1:17-18)
- Reverence is to be given to God for His sovereignty. (v17)
- God entrusts ministry to His willing servant. (v18)

DAY 4: Danger of Spiritual Relapse (1 Timothy 1:19-20)
- Keep the faith. (v19)
- Rebelliousness and lack of faith opens you up to the attacks of the enemy. (v20)

DAY 5: *Tilling the Heart*
Q1: Are you serving where God has called you to serve? If, yes where? If, no, explain why not?
Q2: How do you witness to a person who feels unworthy of accepting God's love?
Q3: When and with who have you shared your testimony of how God saved you from past wrongdoings? Explain?
Q4: Has anything ever caused you to stray away from God? If so, what was the situation and how you were restored? If no, why not?
Q5: What is the difference between earthly life and eternal life?

**Flowering in the Promises of God**
"If we confess our sins, he is faithful and just and will forgive us our sins and purify us from all unrighteousness." (1 John 1:9)

**Morning Glory Prayer**
*Heavenly Father, I thank you for the blood of Jesus Christ redeeming me and cleansing me of my wicked ways and appointing me to serve your people according to your Word. Today, as I step out into the mission field of life, strengthen me to serve humbly with kindness and respect to all, so that you will be magnified. In Jesus' name, I pray. Amen.*

**Tending to the Roots**
1 Timothy 1:12-20

**Nourishing with Praise**
Travis Greene – "You Waited"
Donald Lawrence – "Beautiful Feet"
Casey J – "I'm Yours"
Tonex – "Make Me Over"
Deon Kipping – "By Myself"

**Bringing in the Harvest**
Galatians 3:26, Acts 8:3, 1 Thessalonians 1:3, Luke 19:10, Ephe-sians 2:7, Romans 11:36, 2 Corinthians 10:4, 1 Corinthians 5:5

# Week 50

## JESUS, THE RIGHTEOUS JUDGE

**Morning Glory Devotion**
"There is only one Lawgiver and Judge, the one who is able to save and destroy. But you, who are you to judge your neighbor?" (James 4:12)

**Growing in God's Word**
I prayed and prayed; I waited and waited, but still I received no open door or a Word from God. So, in my haste and lack of faith and patience, I took matters into my own hands. I made it happen; I got just what I thought I wanted, plus more. Because of my haste and lack of faith and patience, I opened doors that should have never been opened. I sought to have what I wanted and ended up hurting myself and those involved.

In my life, I have experienced many hardships, and some of them were due to my bad choices. I heard that little voice (the promptings within me) saying, "Woe, be still," but I moved forward anyway to get what I wanted, even though it was not granted or released by God!

The outcome of my selfish choices came at a high price: shame, disappointment, betrayal, anxiety, broken relationships, and financial loss, just to name a few. But, through my tears and humility with a truly repentant heart, the door of God's grace was opened, which delivered me out of my destructive ways, healing me and giving me a new heart after God. I now want my desires to be what God desires for me. I now pray and wait to be led by the Holy Spirit. I no longer submit myself to the lusts of the world.

I know that, in my haste, I brought judgment upon myself and from others by not waiting on God's timing.

God knows when, where, and what is best for us. A delay is not *no*, but it means if you get it now it will bring you harm (you're not ready for it yet)! I strongly recommend waiting on the perfect time that is God's timing, which comes without sorrow.

**Digging Deeper in the Word** (James 4:1-12)

DAY 1: Selfish Request (James 4:1-3)
- There is a war within us: Flesh vs. Spirit (v1)
- You seek destructive ways to possess things not granted by God. (v2)
- Your request is denied because of selfish desires. (v3)

DAY 2: Worldly Living Hinders the Holy Spirit (James 4:4-6)
- The love of the world is hatred toward God. (v4)
- Lust for the world grieves the Holy Spirit. (v5)
- The grace of God through the Holy Spirit keeps us humble. (v6)

DAY 3: Return to Your First Love (James 4:7-9)
- When you submit you can resist. (v7)
- God is waiting for you. (v8a)
- Repent from all unrighteousness. (v8b)
- Be fully persuaded in your heart and mind. (v8c)
- Declare your heartfelt repentance with sorrow. (v9)

DAY 4: The Judgment Seat Belongs to God (James 4:10-12)
- The meek will be exalted by God. (v10)
- Don't speak curses or condemn your brother for the same will come to you. (v11)
- When you condemn, you claim authority that is reserved for God only. (v12)

DAY 5: *Tilling the Heart*
Q1: How have you been selfish in your prayers?
Q2: Is there any lust for the world within you that may be grieving the Holy Spirit? Explain?

Q3: What areas in your life that you haven't submitted to god yet?
Q4: Why should we not judge anyone?
Q5: Who has the authority to judge? And why?

## Flowering in the Promises of God
"For the revelation awaits an appointed time; it speaks of the end and will not prove false. Though it linger, wait for it; it will certainly come and will not delay." (Habakkuk 2:3)

## Morning Glory Prayer
*Heavenly Father, as I wait for the petitions of my heart, I will wait patiently for the release of your promises. Keep my mind and my heart steadfast on you; open my spiritual ears to hear the promptings of the Holy Spirit. Give me obedient feet to follow your desires for me. Father, judge my motives and remove anything that grieves the Holy Spirit. Empower me to resist the lusts of this world through my submission to you. In Jesus' name I pray, Amen.*

## Tending to the Roots
James 4:1-12

## Nourishing with Praise
John Waller – "While I'm Waiting"
Anthony Evans – "Forgive Me"
J. Moss – "Forgive Me, Lord"
Kevin LeVar – "A Heart that Forgives"
Mali Music – "Make Me New"

## Bringing in the Harvest
Titus 3:9, 1 John 3:15, 1 John 3:22, Matthew 6:24, Numbers 23:19, 1 Peter 5:5, Ephesians 4:27, Zechariah 1:3, Proverbs 14:13, Job 5:11, Romans 14:4, Isaiah 33:22

# Week 51

## GOD COMFORTS US IN OUR SORROW

**Morning Glory Devotion**
"Precious in the sight of the Lord is the death of his faithful servants." (Psalms 116:15)

**Growing in God's Word**
This scripture demonstrates how much God cares for us in death, just like a mother who cares for her child in life.

One day, as my husband was driving from church, he noticed a person sitting in the cemetery. He felt the prompting of the Holy Spirit to stop and offer words of comfort, and in doing so, he found a divorced mother grieving the recent death of her only child and a father who had committed suicide years earlier.

This young Christian woman, gripped with grief, was contemplating suicide. She proclaimed her love for Christ, her trust in Christ, and because of this love she felt compelled through her grief to join her daughter and father in Heaven.

As my husband observed the heaviness of her agony and heard her deep sorrow, he comforted her with words of encouragement and prayer.

Through the comfort of the Holy Spirit she was able to find the strength to live another day. God was attentive to her cries, and through His grace, God revived her will to live and liberated her mind from sorrow to a mind of thanksgiving and praise.

**Digging Deeper in the Word (Psalms 116:1-19)**

DAY 1: God's Attentiveness to Our Call (Psalms 116:1-5)
- I Love the Lord! He hears my cries. (v1)
- I'm devoted to Him for the rest of my life. (v2)
- The emotions felt when facing the reality of death can be overwhelming. (v3)
- Whenever you call on the name of the Lord, you shall be saved. (v4)
- God is righteousness, grace, and compassion. (v5)

DAY 2: Revived by God's Grace (Psalms 116:6-9)
- God meets me in my lowliness. (v6)
- Rest in God's goodness. (v7)
- Under God's protection He restores my life. (v8-9)

DAY 3: State of Mind: Transitioning from Sorrow to Thanksgiving (Ps. 116:10-15)
- Even in my distress I proclaim my trust in Him. (v10)
- In my disappointment, I judge too quickly. (v11)
- We are indebted to the Lord for salvation. (v12-13)
- I will proclaim God's goodness to all. (v14)
- God values the death of his saints. (v15)

DAY 4: The Praises of a Free Man (Psalms 116:16-19)
- We are repositioned from slave to servant. (v16)
- We show our devotion in thanksgiving. (v17)
- We proclaim the continuous testimony of God's goodness. (v18)
- We offer continuous praises in the house of the Lord. (v19)

DAY 5: *Tilling the Heart*
Q1: How do you respond to the death of a loved one?
Q2: Describe a time when you have been rescued by God?
Q3: What helps you to overcome grief and sorrow? Explain.
Q4: How would you explain Psalms 116:19?
Q5: How do you comfort those who are in deep sorrow?

**Flowering in the Promises of God**
"The righteous cry out, and the Lord hears them; he delivers them from all their troubles. The Lord is close to the broken-hearted and saves those who are crushed in spirit. The righteous person may have many troubles, but the Lord delivers him from them all." (Psalms 34:17-19)

**Morning Glory Prayer**
*Heavenly Father, you heard my cry and rescued my life. Your compassion and love comforts my grieving heart. Under your protection, I find rest, restoring my soul. In all my distresses your goodness is there, filling me up with your glory divine. In Jesus' name, I pray. Amen.*

**Tending to the Roots**
Psalms 116:1-19

**Nourishing with Praise**
Plumb (How many times) – "Need You Now"
Tasha Cobbs Leonard – "Gracefully Broken"
Deon Kipping – "By Myself"
Kurt Carr – "I Almost Let Go"
Mary Mary – "Can't Give Up Now"
We Are Messengers – "Point to You"

**Bringing in the Harvest**
Psalms 66:19, Psalms 31:2, Psalms 18:4, Psalms 18:6, Exodus 34:6, Proverbs 1:4, Matthew 11:29, 2 Corinthians 4:13, Romans 3:4, 1 Thessalonians 3:9, Psalms 135:2

# Week 52

## CHRISTIAN UNITY

**Morning Glory Devotion**
"As a prisoner for the Lord, then, I urge you to live a life worthy of the calling you have received. Be completely humble and gentle; be patient, bearing with one another in love." (Ephesians 4:1-2)

**Growing in God's Word**
Often, sharing the Word of God is not just through words; it's connected to our actions. While shopping at the grocery store, I passed an older woman walking down the aisle in the opposite direction from me. I could see the stress in her face and I felt the pulling of my heart prompted by the Holy Spirit to pray for her, so, without hesitation I approached her and said, "Excuse me, ma'am; would it be okay if I prayed for you?" She immediately said yes and that she really need it because she had been going through so much lately and needed all the prayers she could get! I responded by saying, "God knows our hearts, let's pray." "Right now?" she asked, surprised, followed by a gentle nod of *yes*. I placed my hand on her shoulder and prayed for her fervently. At the end of the prayer she looked up at me with tears in her eyes and said, "So many people have said they would pray for me, but you are the only one who actually took time to pray with me, and I know God sent you to me because only God knew the heaviness of my heart." She hugged me and thanked me for praying with her at that moment and for being an obedient Child of God.

How do you show the grace of God to others? Do you have the zeal and the sense of urgency to share the good news of God's saving grace and His love for us? When you witness to the unsaved, are you showing the same mercy and grace that was shown to you? Or are you using the Word of God as a weapon to beat up sinners?

Our approach when witnessing to the unsaved or the brokenhearted will either draw them to Christ or repel them. We should let our witnessing reflect God's character of humbleness, gentleness, patience and love.

God has appointed us to share the gospel in truth so that others will come to know the fullness of Christ. Let's be ready to help others with instant prayer and continue to operate in love for the kingdom of God. Effective witnessing is spreading the gospel and serving people in humility.

**Digging Deeper in the Word** (Ephesians 4:1-16)

DAY 1: The Call of God Manifested in the Lives of Christians (Ephesians 4:1-7)
- Let your Christian life reflect the calling of God. (v1)
- Be humble, gentle, patient, and loving in the fulfillment of your calling. (v2)
- The lack of godly character jeopardizes the unity and peace in the Spirit of the body of Christ. (v3)
- There is one body (Church): a single visible community of faith. (v4a)
- There is one hope for our salvation. (v4b)
- Our allegiance, our commitment, our acceptance, which is Christ. (v5)
- God is omnipresent, omnipotent, and omniscient. (v6)
- Each member of the community of believers shares in God's grace. (v7)

DAY 2: Redemptive Power of Christ (Ephesians 4:8-10)
- From the throne, He liberated the captives. (v8)
- He went to Hell and preached the Gospel to the prisoners. (v9)
- He is the fulfillment of scriptures. (v10)

DAY 3: The Gifts of Ministries Function in the Body of Christ (Ephesians 4:11-13)
- The appointments of the ministry are gifts of grace for the church. (v11)
- The aim of ministry for the church is service. (v12)
- The end result of the ministry is salvation. (v13)

DAY 4: Maturity in the Body of Christ (Ephesians 4:14-16)
- The spiritual development of the believer is the responsibility of the church. (v14)
- The church must maintain the integrity of the Gospel. (v15)
- The church must effectively operate in love. (v16)

DAY 5: *Tilling the Heart*
Q1: What has God call you to do in ministry?
Q2: How would you explain Ephesians 4:5?
Q3: What is the purpose of the different gifts of ministry?
Q4: How do you assess your spiritual development?
Q5: When has your witnessing been ineffective? How did you react?

**Flowering in the Promises of God**
"But when he, the Spirit of truth, comes, he will guide you into all the truth. He will not speak on his own; he will speak only what he hears, and he will tell you what is yet to come." (John 16:13)

**Morning Glory Prayer**
*Heavenly Father, teach me to be effective in witnessing to others about your saving grace. Give me the fortitude to fulfill the calling of the ministry you have appointed me to with humbleness and love. I will share the Word of God with all biblical truths. In Jesus' name, I pray. Amen.*

**Tending to the Roots**
Ephesians 4:1-16

**Nourishing with Praise**
Hezekia Walker – "I need you to Survive"
Babbie Mason – "Standing in the Gap"
Amy Grant – "They Will Know We Are Christians"
Gaither Vocal Band – "We Are All God's Children"

Crowder ft. Tauren Wells – "All My Hope"

**Bringing in the Harvest**
Romans 11:29, Colossians 3:12, Colossians 3:14, 1 Corinthians 12:4, 1 Corinthians 8:6, Romans 11:36, 1 Corinthians 12:11, Colossians 2:15, John 3:13, Hebrews 4:14, 1 Corinthians 12:28, Ephesians 1:23, John 1:16, James 1:6, Colossians 2:19

# ACKNOWLEDGMENTS

God has enriched and surrounded my life with true love and faithful prayers in action from so many people throughout the many stages of my life. As a young girl dealing with major illness, a wife suffering spousal abuse, a divorcee enduring abandonment, a single mother with limited income, my struggles were real but so was my support system of family, friends, sisters, and brothers in Christ, and the unknown names whose charity strengthened my hope for a better tomorrow. Many of you have witnessed my transformation from struggles to victory. I thank you with the love of God for your outpouring of selfless support! Christ Jesus, my greatest love transformed my life with divine healing of mind, spirit, and soul.

To my husband, Greg, your love throughout this process has been demonstrated beautifully through your patience, selfless service, and prayers, and through your countless hours spent explaining the scriptures to me in greater depth. Your desk-side teaching and advising ensured that the Word of God was applied correctly. My love, you never doubted my potential, and your excitement as you watched me write had a tremendous impact on me, pushing me to persevere to completion. You helped me birth this book.

To our beautiful daughters, Ebony, Brittany, Jasmine, Camille, thank you for allowing me to share your stories and for your support of love, prayers, and encouragement. I carry and cherish you all in my heart with great love.

To our grandsons—the (4 C's) Chase, Cam'Ron, Cay'Den, Christian—thank you for sharing your Nana time during my visits, which allowed me to continue to write. The joy and cheers of excitement you all expressed confirmed that the best gift I could ever give you is learning to apply God's Word to your life through my life's experience, to fulfill your godly purpose, to let God's word guide you through life, to have a personal relationship God, and to live a faithful and righteous life that honors God.

Mom and Dad, thank you for raising my siblings and me to have a reverence and love for God. I love you both dearly.

To my publisher, Cara, thank you for hearing my heart and helping me put it into words. Thank you for expressing your love for God's Word through your gift of composing words.

To Rita, the author of *God's Daughters and Their Almost Happily Ever Afters*, thank you for your recommendations that started me on my journey and for blessing this book through your prayers and personal words of love.

Ebony, thank you for the song selections; your praise is your weaponry.

To Ladies Adorned by Christ & Empowered (LACE) Sisters, thank you for your readiness to intercede in prayer and your unity of love.

Thank you, all for being a part of my life's journey.